60 Quick Knits

20 HATS ✻ 20 SCARVES ✻ 20 MITTENS IN CASCADE 220™

sixth&spring
books

sixth&spring books

161 Avenue of the Americas, New York, New York 10013
sixthandspringbooks.com

Managing Editor
WENDY WILLIAMS

Senior Editor
MICHELLE BREDESON

Book Editor
TANIS GRAY

Art Director
DIANE LAMPHRON

Instructions Editor
PAT HARSTE

Instructions Proofreader
THERESE
CHYNOWETH

Technical Illustrations
JANE FAY

Photography
JACK DEUTSCH

Stylist
SARAH LIEBOWITZ

Hair and Makeup
KATIE WEDLUND

Vice President,
Publisher
TRISHA MALCOLM

Creative Director
JOE VIOR

Production Manager
DAVID JOINNIDES

President
ART JOINNIDES

Library of Congress Control Number: 2009941354
ISBN: 978-1-933027-97-5
Manufactured in China
7 9 10 8 6

cascadeyarns.com

contents

Introduction

Ask a group of knitters what their favorite yarn is, and chances are more than a few will say Cascade 220. One of the most popular yarns on the market, Cascade 220 attracts a devoted following, and it all started with a dream of making quality wool affordable.

In the late 1980s Bob and Jean Dunbabin founded Cascade Yarns in the Pioneer Square district of Seattle, Washington. At the time, many knitters were using acrylic yarns, as there were few options for knitters who wanted to use wool; expensive imported merino or coarse wool were the commonly available choices. The Dunbabins believed that if given a chance, people would prefer to knit with wool.

Bob's search for a soft yet affordable wool brought him to Peru. At the time, Peru was not known worldwide for its wool, although Peruvian natives raised sheep that were a blend of Merino and Corriedale in the mountains above 12,000 feet. Bob realized that this soft, long stapled wool was exactly what he was looking for. It was plentiful, light in color and had a tremendous amount of loft.

Largely by word-of-mouth, Cascade 220 became renowned as the affordable, high-quality, worsted weight knitting yarn with great yardage. The popularity of Cascade 220 grew, as did the variety of colors available. There are over two hundred fifty colors in the flagship Cascade 220 line alone, as well as all the colors in Cascade 220 Tweed, Cascade 220 Superwash and Cascade 220 Paints. Now the yarn is available in almost every color imaginable.

While Cascade Yarns has grown tremendously since its start two decades ago, Bob and Jean Dunbabin´s mission remains unchanged: to provide a high-quality product at a price that most knitters can afford. Cascade's insistence upon quality has led to numerous upgrades in spinning machinery, dye kettles and finishing works. True to its goal, Cascade Yarns continues to provide both value and quality.

In this volume of all-new projects, many of today's top knitwear designers come together to create a huge collection of stunning accessories knit in Cascade 220. You'll find dozens of wonderful projects for men, women and kids:

■ Warm your head with a cabled scarf hat with fringe, an adorable monkey hat or a demure heather gray tied cap. ■ Wrap yourself in dazzling scarves, such as a mosaic pattern scarf in multiple blues and greens, a classic garter stitch and basketweave muffler or a multicolored scarf with a ruffle that runs its entire length. ■ Keep your hands cozy with heather green fingerless mittens with a delicate leaf motif, kids' mitts with a fun octopus design or Fair Isle flower mittens with striped cuffs.

Whether you're knitting for yourself or looking for sure-to-please gift ideas, you'll find plenty of wonderful designs to choose from.

✻ To locate retailers that carry Cascade 220, visit cascadeyarns.com.

❋ Things to Know

Abbreviations

approx	approximately
beg	begin(ning)
CC	contrasting color
ch	chain
cm	centimeter(s)
cn	cable needle
cont	continu(e)(ing)
dec	decreas(e)(ing)
dpn	double-pointed needle(s)
foll	follow(s)(ing)
g	gram(s)
inc	increas(e)(ing)
k	knit
LH	left-hand
lp(s)	loop(s)
m	meter(s)
mm	millimeter(s)
MC	main color
M1	make 1 (knit stitch)
M1 p-st	make 1 purl stitch
oz	ounce(s)
p	purl
pat(s)	pattern(s)
pm	place marker
psso	pass slip stitch(es) over
rem	remain(s)(ing)
rep	repeat
RH	right-hand
RS	right side(s)

rnd(s)	round(s)
SKP	slip 1, knit 1, pass slip stitch over—one stitch has been decreased
SK2P	slip 1, knit 2 together, pass slip stitch over the knit 2 together—two stitches have been decreased
S2KP	slip 2 stitches together, knit 1, pass 2 slip stitches over knit 1
sl	slip
sl st	slip stitch
ssk	slip, slip, knit
sssk	slip, slip, slip, knit
st(s)	stitch(es)
St st	stockinette stitch
tbl	through back loop(s)
tog	together
WS	wrong side(s)
wyib	with yarn in back
wyif	with yarn in front
yd	yard(s)
yo	yarn over needle
*	repeat directions following * as many times as indicated
[ ]	repeat directions inside brackets as many times as indicated

Knitting Needles

U.S.	Metric
0	2mm
1	2.25mm
2	2.75mm
3	3.25mm
4	3.5mm
5	3.75mm
6	4mm
7	4.5mm
8	5mm
9	5.5mm
10	6mm
10½	6.5mm
11	8mm
13	9mm
15	10mm
17	12.75mm
19	15mm
35	19mm

Checking Your Gauge

Make a test swatch at least 4"/10cm square. If the number of stitches and rows does not correspond to the gauge given, you must change the needle size. An easy rule to follow is: To get fewer stitches to the inch/cm, use a larger needle; to get more stitches to the inch/cm, use a smaller needle. Continue to try different needle sizes until you get the same number of stitches in the gauge.

Skill Levels

BEGINNER — Ideal first project.

EASY — Basic stitches, minimal shaping and simple finishing.

INTERMEDIATE — For knitters with some experience. More intricate stitches, shaping and finishing.

EXPERIENCED — For knitters able to work patterns with complicated shaping and finishing.

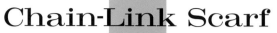

Chain-Link Scarf

This lengthwise-knit ring-motif scarf will have you feeling loopy. Deep purple variegated yarn creates a rich background for the black chain pattern.

DESIGNED BY LOIS YOUNG

■■■□
INTERMEDIATE

Finished measurements
Approx 7½" x 58½"/19cm x 148.5cm

Materials
■ 2 3½oz/100g hanks (each approx 220yd/201m) of Cascade Yarns *220 Paints* (Peruvian highland wool) in #9871 grape (MC)

■ 1 3½oz/100g hank (each approx 220yd/201m) of Cascade Yarns *220 Wool* (Peruvian highland wool) in #8555 black (CC)

■ One pair size 7 (4.5mm) needles *or size to obtain gauge*

Notes
1) Scarf is knit horizontally from one long edge to opposite long edge.
2) Circular needle is used to accommodate the large number of sts. Do not join, but work back and forth in rows.
3) Color changes are made in the last stitch of a row. To change colors, work to last st, bring up new color yarn from under old color, then k1 tbl in last st with new color.
4) Carry color not in use loosely along side edge of work.

Scarf
With MC, loosely cast on 264 sts.

BORDER
Next row With MC, sl 1, k to end. Rep last row 3 times more.
Next row With MC, sl 1, k to last st, bring up CC from under MC, then k1 tbl in last st with CC. Cont in pat st as foll:
Row 1 (RS) With CC, sl 1, k to end.
Row 2 With CC, k to last st, change to MC, k1 tbl.
Row 3 With MC, sl 1, k2, *sl 2 wyib, k6; rep from *, end last rep k3 (instead of k6).
Row 4 With MC, sl 1, k2, *sl 2 wyif, p6; rep from * to last 5 sts, end sl 2 wyif,

k2, change to CC, k1 tbl.
Row 5 With CC, sl 1, k2, *sl 2 wyib, k6; rep from *, end last rep k3 (instead of k6).
Row 6 With CC, sl 1, k to last st, change to MC, k1 tbl.
Row 7 With MC, sl 1, k to end of row.
Rows 8 With MC, sl 1, k2, p to last 3 sts, end k2, change to CC, k1 tbl.
Row 9 Rep row 1.
Row 10 Rep row 2.
Row 11 With MC, k7, *sl 2 wyib, k6; rep from *, end last rep k7 (instead of k6).
Row 12 With MC, k3, p4, *sl 2 wyif, p6; rep from * to last 9 sts, end sl 2 wyif, p4, k2, change to CC, k1 tbl.
Row 13 With CC, k7, *sl 2 wyib, k6; rep from *, end last rep k7 (instead of k6).
Row 14 Rep row 6.
Row 15 Rep row 7.
Row 16 Rep row 8. Rep rows 1–16 twice more, then rows 1–8 once.

BORDER
Next row With MC, sl 1, k to end. Rep last row 4 times more. Bind off all sts loosely knitwise.

Finishing
Block piece to measurements. ■

Gauge
18 sts and 34 rows to 4"/10cm over pat st using size 7 (4.5mm) needles (after blocking).
Take time to check gauge.

Cabled Brim Tam

Top off your look with this bold beauty. The band is knit in one long strip, then rotated, and the stitches are picked up along the top, making it easy to size up or down.

DESIGNED BY THERESE CHYNOWETH

INTERMEDIATE

Sizes
Instructions are written for one size.

Finished measurements
Circumference 21"/53.5cm
Depth 10½"/26.5cm

Materials
- 1 3½oz/100g hank (each approx 220yd/201m) of Cascade Yarns *220 Wool* (Peruvian highland wool) in #9487 puget sound
- Contrasting heavy worsted-weight yarn (waste yarn)
- Size 7 (4.5mm) circular needle, 16"/40cm length *or size to obtain gauge*
- One set (5) size 7 (4.5mm) double-pointed needles (dpns)
- Cable needle (cn)
- Size G/6 (4mm) crochet hook (for chain-st provisional cast-on)
- Stitch markers

Stitch glossary
4-st RPC Sl 1 st to cn and hold to *back*, k3, p1 from cn.
4-st LPC Sl 3 sts to cn and hold to *front*, p1, k3 from cn.

6-st RC Sl 3 sts to cn and hold to *back*, k3, k3 from cn.
6-st LC Sl 3 sts to cn and hold to *front*, k3, k3 from cn.

Hat
BRIM
With crochet hook and waste yarn, ch 30 for chain-st provisional cast-on. Cut yarn and draw end though lp on hook. Turn ch so bottom lps are at top and cut end is at left. With dpn and main yarn, beg 2 lps from right end, pick up and k 1 st in each of next 26 lps.

Beg chart pat
Row 1 (WS) Beg at st 26 and work to st 1. Working back and forth on 2 dpns, cont to foll chart in this way to row 16, then rep rows 1–16. AT THE SAME TIME, on first row 2, mark beg of this RS row to indicate top edge of brim. When piece measures approx 21"/53.5cm from beg, end with row 15. With RS facing, release cut end from lp of waste yarn ch. Pulling out 1 ch at a time, place live sts on a dpn. Graft ends tog using Kitchener st or 3-needle bind-off, forming a ring.

SIDES
With WS facing and circular needle, pick up and knit 96 sts evenly spaced around top edge of brim. Turn work to RS. Join and pm for beg of rnds.
Next rnd [K16, pm] 5 times, k16. Cont to work in pat sts as foll:
Rnds 1 and 3 *K1 tbl, p to marker; rep from * around.
Rnd 2 *Sl 1 wyib, [k2, M1] 7 times, k1; rep from * around—138 sts.
Rnds 4, 6 and 8 *Sl 1 wyib, k to marker; rep from * around.
Rnd 5 *K1 tbl, p3, [M1, p4] 4 times, M1, p3; rep from * around—168 sts.
Rnd 7 *K1 tbl, p to marker; rep from * around.

Gauges
18 sts and 39 rows to 4"/10 cm over garter st using size 7 (4.5mm) needle. 26 sts to 3½"/9 cm over chart pat using size 7 (4.5mm) dpns. *Take time to check gauges.*

Cabled Brim Tam

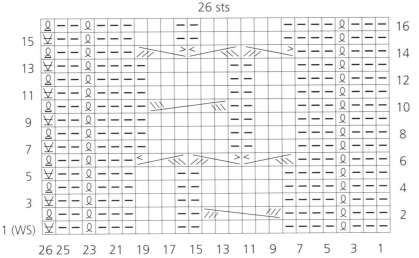

26 sts

15 ... 16 (right side numbers 16,14,12,10,8,6,4,2)
1 (WS) ... left numbers 15,13,11,9,7,5,3

26 25 23 21 19 17 15 13 11 9 7 5 3 1

Yarn Smarts

It's best to wash knitted wool items by hand in cold water with a gentle soap made especially for wool.

Stitch Key

☐ K on RS, p on WS

— P on RS, k on WS

Ⅵ K tbl on RS, p tbl on WS

Ⅵ P tbl on RS

Ⅴ S1 st purlwise wyib on WS

4-st RPC

4-st LPC

6-st RC

6-st LC

CROWN SHAPING

Change to dpns (dividing sts evenly between 4 needles) when there are too few sts on circular needle.

Rnd 9 *K1 tbl, p2tog, p to 2 sts before marker, p2tog; rep from * around—156 sts.

Rnd 10 *Sl 1 wyib, k to marker; rep from * around.

Rnd 11 *K1 tbl, p to marker; rep from * around.

Rnd 12 *Sl 1 wyib, k2tog, k to 2 sts before marker, k2tog; rep from * around—144 sts.

Rnd 13 *K1 tbl, p to marker; rep from * around.

Rnd 14 *Sl 1 wyib, k to marker; rep from * around.

Rnds 15–32 Rep rnds 9–14 3 times—72 sts.

Rnd 33 *K1 tbl, p2tog, p to 2 sts before marker, p2tog; rep from * around—60 sts.

Rnds 34 and 36 *Sl 1 wyib, k to marker; rep from * around.

Rnd 35 *K1 tbl, p to marker; rep from * around.

Rnd 37–44 Rep rnds 33–36 twice—36 sts.

Rnd 45 *K1 tbl, p2tog, p to 2 sts before marker, p2tog; rep from * around—24 sts.

Rnds 46, 48 and 50 *Sl 1 wyib, k to marker; rep from * around.

Rnds 47 and 49 *K1 tbl, p to marker; rep from * around.

Rnd 51 *K1 tbl, p3tog; rep from * around—12 sts.

Rnds 52 and 54 *Sl 1 wyib, k to marker; rep from * around.

Rnd 53 *K1 tbl, p to marker; rep from * around.

Rnd 55 [K2tog] 6 times—6 sts.

Rnd 56 Knit. Cut yarn, leaving an 8"/20.5cm tail and thread through rem sts. Pull tog tightly and secure end. ■

Waffle Mittens

These waffle-knit mittens are so yummy you'll eat them right up. With simple styling and an easy stitch pattern, they knit up quicker than you can say "pass the syrup"!

DESIGNED BY CHERYL MURRAY

Sizes
Instructions are written for one size.

Finished measurements
Hand circumference 7½"/19cm
Length of cuff approx 2¾"/7cm

Materials
■ 1 3½oz/100g hank (each approx 220yd/201m) of Cascade Yarns *220 Wool* (Peruvian highland wool) in #9499 sand
■ One set (5) each size 6 and 8 (4 and 5mm) double-pointed needles (dpns) *or size to obtain gauge*
■ Stitch markers
■ Tapestry needle

Note
To work in the rnd, always read charts from right to left.

Stitch glossary
M1 k-st With the needle tip, lift the strand between the last st worked and the next st on the LH needle and knit it.

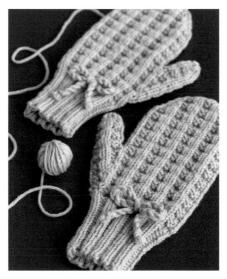

M1 p-st With the needle tip, lift the strand between the last st worked and the next st on the LH needle and purl it.

Basketweave pattern
Rnds 1 and 2 Knit.
Rnds 3 and 4 K1, *p2, k2; rep from * around to last st, end k1.
Rep rnds 1–4 for basketweave pat.

Mittens (make 2)
CUFF
With smaller dpns, cast on 40 sts.

Divide sts over 4 needles (10 sts on each). Join, taking care not to twist sts on needles, pm for beg of rnds. Work in k2, p2 rib as foll:
Rnd 1 K1, *p2, k2; rep from * around to last st, end k1. Rep this rnd until piece measures 2¾"/7cm from beg. Change to larger dpns and work rnds 1 and 2 of basketweave pat. Cont in basketweave pat as foll:

THUMB GUSSET
Next rnd Work rnd 3 over first 19 sts, in next st work (k1, pm, p1), in next st work (p1, pm, k1), *p2, k2; rep from * around to last st, end k1—42 sts.
Note The 2 increased sts between markers beg thumb gusset.
Beg chart I
Rnd 1 Work rnd 4 of basketweave pat to first marker, sl marker, foll chart I over next 2 sts to 2nd marker, work rnd 4 of basketweave pat to end. Keeping 20 sts each side of thumb gusset markers in basketweave pat, cont to foll chart in this way. Continue working in Basketweave pattern, following chart I for stitches between markers, to rnd 18—52 sts (12 sts between markers).

Gauge
20 sts and 31 rnds to 4"/10cm over basketweave pat using larger dpns.
Take time to check gauge.

Waffle Mittens

Chart I

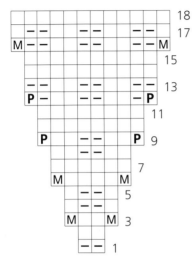

Chart II

Stitch Key

☐ K on RS

− P on RS

M M1 k-st

P M1 p-st

↗ K2tog

↘ Ssk

Next rnd Work in basketweave pat to first marker, drop marker, place next 12 sts on scrap yarn for thumb, drop marker, work in basketweave pat to end—40 sts. Cont in basketweave pat until piece measures approx 5½"/14cm above ribbing, end with rnd 4.

TOP SHAPING
Beg chart II
Work rnds 1–12, working decs as indicated—8 sts. Cut yarn, leaving a 12"/30.5cm tail. Place 4 sts from front on one needle and 4 sts from back on a 2nd needle. Graft sts tog using Kitchener st or 3-needle bind-off.

THUMB
Remove waste yarn and place 12 live sts on larger dpns, dividing sts over 3 needles (4 sts on each). Join yarn, leaving a long tail for sewing. Join and pm for beg of rnds. Work even in basketweave pat for 1¾"/4.5cm.

TOP SHAPING
Dec rnd 1 [K2tog, k2] 3 times—9 sts. Work next rnd even.
Dec rnd 2 [K2tog, k1] 3 times—6 sts. Cut yarn, leaving a 6"/15cm tail. Thread tail in tapestry needle, then thread through rem sts. Pull tog tightly and secure end. Use yarn tail at base of thumb to close up any gaps between thumb and hand.

Twisted cords (make 2)
Cut a 40"/101.5cm strand of yarn. Fold in half, then knot cut ends together. Holding the knot in your hand, slip the loop over a hook and pull tight. Slip a pencil through the knotted end, then rotate the pencil, twisting the cord until it starts to double back on itself. Put one finger in center of cord and carefully fold in half, letting two ends of cord twist together. Knot ends to secure twist. On back of mitten, thread cord through center 2 sts just above last row of ribbing. Tie into a bow, then adjust to desired bow size. Re-knot ends approx 1½"/4cm from base of bow, then trim off excess yarn ¼"/.5cm from knots. ■

Puppy Mittens

Your little one will hound you to make these super-cute mittens. Change the body, ear or tail colors to match your favorite pooch!

DESIGNED BY SHERRY GRAZIANO

EASY

Sizes
Instructions for Child size Small. Changes for Medium are in parentheses.

Finished measurements
Hand circumference
5¼ (6)"/13.5 (15)cm
Length of cuff approx 3"/7.5cm

Materials
■ 1 3½oz/100g ball (each approx 220yd/201m) of Cascade Yarns *220 Superwash* (superwash wool) each in #874 ridge rock (MC) and #1913 jet (CC)

■ One set (5) size 6 (4mm) double-pointed needles (dpns) *or size to obtain gauge*

■ Stitch markers

■ Four ³⁄₈"/9mm shank buttons in brown and black

Stitch glossary
kfb Knit in front and back of st—1 st increased.

Mitten (make 2)
CUFF
With dpns and MC, cast on 32 (36) sts and divide sts evenly over 3 needles.

Join taking care not to twist sts on needles, pm for beg of rnds. Work around in p2, k2 rib as foll:
Rnd 1 P1, k2, *p2, k2; rep from * around, end p1. Rep this rnd until piece measures 3"/7.5cm from beg.

HAND
Next (dec) rnd Knit, dec 3 sts evenly spaced—29 (33) sts. Knit next 2 rnds. Cont in St st as foll:

THUMB GUSSET
Inc rnd 1 K 13 (15), pm, kfb, k1, kfb, pm, k to end—31 (35) sts. Knit next 2 rnds.
Inc rnd 2 K to first marker, sl marker, kfb, k3, kfb, sl marker, k to end—33 (37) sts. Knit next 2 rnds.
Inc rnd 3 K to first marker, sl marker, kfb, k5, kfb, sl marker, k to end—35 (39) sts. Knit next 1 (2) rnds.

FOR MEDIUM SIZE ONLY
Inc rnd 4 K to first marker, sl marker, kfb, k7, kfb, sl marker, k to end—41 sts. Knit next rnd.

FOR BOTH SIZES
Next rnd K to first marker, drop marker, place next 9 (11) sts on scrap yarn, drop marker, k to end—26 (30) sts. Cont in St st until piece measures 5½ (6¼)"/14 (16)cm from beg.

TOP SHAPING
Dec rnd 1 [K2, k2tog] 6 (7) times, k2—20 (23) sts. Knit next 2 rnds.
Dec rnd 2 [K1, k2tog] 6 (7) times, k2—14 (16) sts. Knit next rnd.
Dec rnd 3 [K2tog] 7 (8) times—7 (8) sts.
Dec rnd 4 K 1 (0), [k2tog] 3 (4) times—4 sts. Cut yarn, leaving a 6"/15cm tail and thread through rem sts. Pull tog tightly and secure end.

THUMB
Place 9 (11) thumb gusset sts over 2 needles.
Next rnd Join MC and knit across sts, then pick up and k 2 sts at base of hand—11 (13) sts. Divide sts evenly over 3 needles. Join and pm for beg of rnds. Cont in St st for 1 (1¼)"/2.5 (3)cm.

TOP SHAPING
Dec rnd 1 [K1, k2tog] 3 (4) times, k 2 (1) —8 (9) sts. Knit next rnd.
Dec rnd 2 [K2tog] 4 times, k 0 (1) —4 (5) sts. Cut yarn, leaving a 6"/15cm tail and thread through rem sts. Pull tog tightly and secure end.

Ears (make 4)
Beg at base of ear, with dpns and CC, cast on 5 sts. Working back and forth on 2 needles, work in garter st for 11 rows. (Continued on page 160.)

Gauge
20 sts and 28 rnds to 4"/10cm over St st using size 6 (4mm) dpns. *Take time to check gauge.*

Tweed Watch Cap

Cables and garter ridges have this manly hat going every which way.
Add extra dimension with myriad colors or multiple tweeds.

DESIGNED BY LYNN WILSON

INTERMEDIATE

Sizes
Instructions are written for one size.

Finished measurements
Circumference 19½"/49.5cm
Depth 8½"/21.5cm

Materials
■ 1 3½oz/100g hank (each approx 220yd/201m) of Cascade Yarns *220 Wool Heathers* (Peruvian highland wool) each in #8013 walnut heather (A) and #9332 sapphire (B) and #9325 west point blue heather (C)

■ Sizes 7 and 8 (4.5 and 5mm) circular needles, 16"/40cm length *or size to obtain gauge*

■ One set (5) size 7 (4.5mm) double-pointed needles (dpns)

■ Stitch marker

Stitch glossary
RT (right twist) Skip first stitch on LH needle and knit into 2nd stitch, then knit into the skipped stitch and slip both stitches off needle.

Hat
With smaller circular needle and A, loosely cast on 100 sts. Join and pm taking care not to twist sts on needle. Cont in pat sts as foll:

Rnds 1, 3, 5 Purl.
Rnds 2 and 4 Knit. Change to larger circular needle.
Rnds 6 and 7 With B, *k1, sl 1 wyib; rep from * around.
Rnd 8 With A, knit.
Rnd 9 With A, purl.
Rnds 10 and 11 With C, *k1, sl 1 wyib; rep from * around.
Rnd 12 With A, knit.
Rnd 13 With A, purl.
Rnds 14 and 15 With B, *k1, sl 1 wyib; rep from * around.
Rnd 16 With A, knit.
Rnd 17 With A, purl. Change to smaller circular needle.
Rnd 18 With A, knit.
Rnd 19 With A, purl.
Rnd 20 With A, *RT, k3; rep from * around.
Rnd 21 With A, *k2, p3; rep from * around.
Rnd 22 With C, *sl 2 wyib, k3; rep from * around.
Rnd 23 With C, *sl 2 wyib, p3; rep from * around.
Rnd 24 With A, *RT, k3; rep from * around.
Rnd 25 With A, *k2, p3; rep from * around.
Rnd 26 With B, *sl 2 wyib, k3; rep from * around.
Rnd 27 With B, *sl 2 wyib, p3; rep from * around. Rep rnds 20–27 5 times more, then rnd 20 once.

CROWN SHAPING
Change to dpns (dividing sts evenly between 4 needles) when there are too few sts on circular needle.
Rnd 28 With A, *k2, p2tog, p1; rep from * around—80 sts.
Rnd 29 With C, *sl 2, k2; rep from * around.
Rnd 30 With C, *sl 2, p2; rep from * around.
Rnd 31 With A, *RT, k2; rep from * around.
Rnd 32 With A, *k2, p2; rep from * around.
Rnd 33 With B, *sl 2, k2; rep from * around.
Rnd 34 With B, *sl 2, p2; rep from * around.
Rnd 35 With A, *RT, k2; rep from * around.
Rnd 36 With A, *k2, p2tog; rep from * around—60 sts.
Rnd 37 With C, *sl 2, k1; rep from * around.
Rnd 38 With C, *sl 2, p1; rep from * around. Cut C.
Rnd 39 With A, *RT, k1; rep from * around.
Rnd 40 With A, *k2, p1; rep from * around.
Rnd 41 With B, *sl 2, k1; rep from * around.
Rnd 42 With B, *sl 2, p1; rep from * around. Cut B.
Rnd 43 With A, *k1, ssk; rep from * around—40 sts.
Rnd 44 With A, *k2tog; rep from * around—20 sts.
Rnd 45 With A, *k2tog; rep from * around—10 sts. Cut A, leaving an 8"/20.5cm tail and thread through rem sts. Pull tog tightly and secure end. ■

Gauge
20 sts and 28 rnds to 4"/10cm over St st using smaller needle. *Take time to check gauge.*

Tied Rectangle Wrap

This menswear-inspired number takes the men's tie and transforms it into an elegant finishing touch for a woman's scarf. It's knit flat in simple rib and seed stitch. Who says style can't be easy?

DESIGNED BY ANGELA JUERGENS

EASY

Finished measurements
Approx 7½" x 38"/19cm x 96.5cm

Materials
■ 2 3½oz/100g hanks (each approx 220yd/201m) of Cascade Yarns *220 Wool Heathers* (Peruvian highland wool) in #9456 sapphire heather

■ Size 7 (4.5mm) circular needle, 29"/74cm length *or size to obtain gauge*

■ Stitch markers

Notes
1) Scarf is knit horizontally from one long edge to opposite long edge.
2) Circular needle is used to accommodate the large number of sts. Do not join, but work back and forth in rows.

K2, P2 rib
(multiple of 4 sts plus 2)
Row 1 (RS) K2, *p2, k2; rep from * to end.
Row 2 P2, *k2, p2; rep from * to end.
Rep rows 1 and 2 for k2, p2 rib.

Seed stitch
(over an even number of sts)
Row 1 (RS) *K1, p1; rep from * to end.
Row 2 K the purl sts and p the knit sts.
Rep row 2 for seed st.

Scarf
Cast on 202 sts. Work in k2, p2 rib until piece measures 5½"/14cm from beg, end with a WS row.

TIES
Next row (RS) Bind off first 52 sts in rib, work in rib to end.
Next row Bind off first 40 sts in rib, work in rib to end, pm, cast on 50 sts using knitting-on method.
Next row Work in seed st to marker, work in rib to end, pm, cast on 38 sts using knitting-on method—198 sts.
Next row Work in seed st to first marker, work in rib to marker, work in seed st to end. Keeping tie sts in seed st and rem sts in rib, work even until piece measures 7½"/19cm from beg. Bind off all sts loosely in pat sts.

Finishing
Block piece lightly to measurements. ■

Gauge
19 sts and 31 rows to 4"/10cm over k2, p2, rib using size 7 (4.5mm) needle.
Take time to check gauge.

Embroidered Mittens

Deck your mitts in fabulous floral embroidery and shimmering beads. With a backdrop of simple stockinette, these mittens take it to another level with tone-on-tone adornment.

DESIGNED BY JULIE GADDY

Sizes
Instructions are written for one size.

Finished measurements
Hand circumference 8"/20.5cm
Length of cuff approx 3"/7.5cm

Materials
■ 1 3½oz/100g hank (each approx 220yd/201m) of Cascade Yarns *220 Wool* (Peruvian highland wool) each in #7810 amethyst (MC) and #7809 violet (CC)

■ One set (4) each size 5 and 7 (3.75 and 4.5mm) double-pointed needles (dpns) *or size to obtain gauge*

■ Stitch marker

■ 14 size 11/0 seed beads

■ Matching sewing thread

■ Sewing needle

Stitch glossary
M1R (make 1 right) Insert left needle from *back* to *front* into the horizontal strand between the last st worked and the next st on left needle. Knit this strand through the front loop to twist the st.
M1L (make 1 left) Insert left needle from *front* to *back* into the horizontal strand between the last st worked and the next st on left needle. Knit this strand through the back loop to twist the st.

Mittens (make 2)
CUFF
With smaller dpns and MC, cast on 40 sts and divide sts evenly over 3 needles. Join, taking care not to twist sts on needles, pm for beg of rnds. Work around in k1, p1 rib for 3"/7.5cm.

HAND
Next (inc) rnd K19, use RH needle to pull up loop of the p st of rnd below and place it on LH needle, k this st, then k st on LH needle, k to end—41 sts. Change to larger dpns and cont in St st for 9 rnds.

THUMB GUSSET
Inc rnd 1 K19, pm, M1L, k2, M1R, pm, k to end—43 sts (4 sts between markers). Knit next rnd.
Inc rnd 2 K to first marker, sl marker, M1L, k to 2nd marker, M1R, sl marker, k to end—45 sts (6 sts between markers). Knit next rnd. Rep last 2 rnds 6 times more—57 sts (18 sts between markers).
Next rnd K to first marker, drop marker, place next 18 sts on scrap yarn for thumb, drop marker, cast on 1 st, k to end—40 sts. Cont in St st until piece measures approx 6¼"/16cm above ribbing.

TOP SHAPING
Dec rnd 1 K18, *slip next 2 sts knitwise, k next st, then pass two slipped sts over*, k17; rep from * to * incorporating first st of next rnd into dec—36 sts. Knit next rnd.
Dec rnd 2 K16, *slip next 2 sts knitwise, k next st, then pass two slipped sts over*, k15; rep from * to * incorporating first st of next rnd into dec—32 sts. Knit next rnd.
Dec rnd 3 K14, *slip next 2 sts knitwise, k next st, then pass two slipped sts over*, k13; rep from * to * incorporating first st of next rnd into dec—28 sts. Knit next rnd.

Gauge
20 sts and 28 rnds to 4"/10cm over St st using larger dpns.
Take time to check gauge.

Embroidered Mittens

LAZY DAISY
STITCH

STEM STITCH

Stitch Key

⬭ Lazy Daisy Stitch

〰 Stem Stitch

◌ Bead

Dec rnd 4 K12, *slip next 2 sts knitwise, k next st, then pass two slipped sts over*, k11; rep from * to * incorporating first st of next rnd into dec—24 sts. Knit next rnd.
Dec rnd 5 K10, *slip next 2 sts knitwise, k next st, then pass two slipped sts over*, k9; rep from * to * incorporating first st of next rnd into dec—20 sts. Knit next rnd. Arrange sts on 2 needles with dec st as first st. Cut yarn leaving a 20"/51cm tail. Graft sts tog using Kitchener st or 3-needle bind-off.

THUMB
Place 18 thumb gusset sts over 2 needles.
Next rnd Join yarn and knit across sts, then pick up and k 1 st in cast-on of thumb opening—19 sts. Divide sts evenly over 3 needles. Join and pm for beg of rnds. Cont in St st for 1½"/4cm.

TOP SHAPING
Dec rnd 1 [K4, k2tog] 3 times, k1—16 sts. Knit next rnd.
Dec rnd 2 [K3, k2tog] 3 times, k1—13 sts. Knit next rnd.

Dec rnd 3 [K2, k2tog) 3 times, k1—10 sts. Knit next rnd.
Dec rnd 4 [K1, k2tog) 3 times, k1—7 sts. Knit next rnd.
Dec rnd 5 [K2tog] 3 times, k1—4 sts. Cut yarn, leaving a 6"/15cm tail and thread through rem sts. Pull tog tightly and secure end.

Finishing

Refer to stitch diagram for design on back of right mitten. For right mitten, work as foll: for 3-petal flower, measure and pin-mark 2½"/6.5cm down from top edge and 1½"/4cm in from RH edge. Pin indicates center of flower. Using CC throughout, embroider 3-petal lazy daisy stitch flower. For 5-petal flower, measure and pin-mark 4¼"/11cm down from top edge and 2¼"/5.5cm in from RH edge. Embroider flower. For leaves, measure and pin-mark 5"/12.5cm up from bottom edge and 3"/7.5cm in from RH edge. Embroider 2-stitch leaves. Connect the flowers and leaves with lines of stem stitch. Using sewing thread, sew 4 seed beads to center of 5-petal flower and 3 beads to center of 3-petal flower. For back of left mitten, measure and pin-mark as for right mitten, measuring in from LH edge. Reverse the position of the flowers and stems to form a mirror image. ■

Lion Scarf

Your youngster will be the mane event in this ferociously cute scarf. A simple seed-stitch body and a fringe-framed face will have him or her roaring with laughter.

DESIGNED BY AMY BAHRT

Finished measurements
Approx 4" x 42"/10cm x 106.5cm

Materials
■ 1 3½oz/100g ball (each approx 220yd/201m) of Cascade Yarns *220 Superwash* (superwash wool) each in #877 tangerine (MC), #841 moss (A) and #886 citron (B)

■ One pair size 6 (4mm) needles *or size to obtain gauge*

■ Size G/6 (4mm) crochet hook

■ Stitch holder

■ Two ½"/12mm 4-hole shirt buttons in white

■ Blue felt

■ Blue sewing thread

■ Small amount of polyester fiberfill

■ Sewing needle

■ Tapestry needle

Seed stitch
(over an even number of sts)
Row 1 (RS) *K1, p1; rep from * to end.
Row 2 K the purl sts and p the knit sts.
Rep row 2 for seed st.

Scarf
HEAD
With MC, cast on 12 sts. Work in seed st for 1 row. Cont in seed st and inc 1 st each side on next row, then every other row 4 times more —22 sts.

BODY
Work even until piece measures 39"/99cm from beg, end with a WS row.

Gauge
21 sts and 37 rows to 4"/10cm over seed st using size 6 (4mm) needles.
Take time to check gauge.

Lion Scarf

LEGS

Next row (RS) Work across first 7 sts, join a 2nd ball of MC and bind off center 8 sts, work to end. Working both legs at once, work even for 2½"/6.5cm, end with a WS row.

PAWS

Change to A and cont in seed st for 7 rows. Bind off each side in seed st.

EARS (make 2)

Beg at bottom edge, with MC, cast on 6 sts. Work in seed st for 4 rows. Cut yarn, leaving a 36"/91.5cm tail and thread through rem sts. Pull tog tightly and secure end; do not cut off excess tail.

Finishing

Block scarf lightly to measurements. To delineate outline of head, fold bottom edge 3"/7.5cm to RS. Using thread doubled in needle, sew a running stitch guideline following curve of bottom edge; unfold.

EARS

For each ear, thread tail in tapestry needle. Weave along side edge to bottom edge. With RS facing, embroider a row of chain stitches along the curved outer edge to opposite bottom edge. Sew on each ear so outer edge is ½"/1.3cm from side edge of head and angled following running stitch guideline.

NOSE

Cut nose from blue felt following actual-size pattern. Position nose 2¼"/5.5cm from bottom edge and centered side to side. Using thread, whip stitch in place along two edges. Stuff lightly with fiberfill, then whip stitch remaining side closed.

EYES

Using thread doubled in needle, sew on buttons, stitching through holes forming an X; as shown.

MANE

Cut approx 66 strands each of A and B, 5"/12.5cm long. Use 1 strand each of A and B for each fringe. Using crochet hook, knot each fringe ¼"/.6cm from outer edge around face, then following guideline before and between ears. Remove thread guideline.

TAIL

Cut 3 strands of MC, 20"/51cm long. From RS, insert crochet hook 2"/5cm up from bound-off sts between legs and centered side to side. Gather the 3 strands tog, ends even, then fold in half. Use hook to pull through folded end, then pull cut ends through fold. Pull on cut ends to tighten knot. Using 3 pairs of strands, braid for 3"/7.5cm. Make an overhand knot at end of braiding. Trim excess yarn leaving 1"/2.5cm extending beyond knot. ■

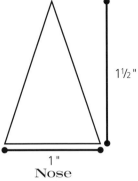

1½"

1"

Nose
Actual Size

CHAIN STITCH

WHIP STITCH

Quick Tip

Make it a family affair! Let your child choose the colors for this scarf. He or she can even help sew on the buttons for the eyes.

Monkey Hat

It's a jungle out there! Keep your little one's head and ears warm with this adorable topper featuring earflaps that secure under the chin with I-cord ties.

DESIGNED BY IRINA POLUDNENKO

INTERMEDIATE

Sizes
Instructions are written for Child size Small.

Finished measurements
Circumference 16"/40.5cm
Depth 5¾"/14.5cm (excluding earflaps)

Materials
■ 1 3½oz/100g ball (each approx 220yd/201m) of Cascade Yarns *220 Superwash* (superwash wool) each in #858 ginger (MC), #853 camel (A) and #815 coal (B)
■ Size 7 (4.5mm) circular needle, 16"/40cm length *or size to obtain gauge*
■ One set (5) size 7 (4.5mm) double-pointed needles (dpns)
■ Stitch holders
■ Stitch markers

Muzzle
With dpns and A, cast on 7 sts. Working back and forth on 2 dpns, cont in garter st as foll:
Inc row 1 (RS) Sl 1, *(k1, yo, k1) in next st, k1; rep from * once more, end (k1, yo, k1) in next st, p1—13 sts. Knit next row.
Inc row 2 (RS) Sl 1, *(k1, yo, k1) in next st, k1; rep from * 4 times more, end (k1, yo, k1) in next st, p1—25 sts. Knit next 24 rows, end with a RS row. Place sts on holder.

Earflaps (make 2)
I-CORD TIE
With dpn and MC, cast on 3 sts, leaving a long tail for sewing. Work in I-cord as foll: ***Next row (RS)** With 2nd dpn, k3, do not turn. Slide sts back to beg of needle to work next row from RS; rep from * until I-cord measures 4½"/11cm from beg.

EARFLAP
Cont to work back and forth in garter st as foll:
Inc row 1 (RS) Sl 1, (k1, yo, k1) in next st, p1—5 sts. Knit next row.
Inc row 2 (RS) Sl 1, k1, M1, k to last 2 sts, end M1, k1, p1—7 sts. Knit next row. Rep last 2 rows 4 times more, then inc row 2 once, end with a RS row—17 sts. Place sts on holder.

Hat
With circular needle and MC, cast on 9 sts using knitting-on method, k17 sts from first earflap holder, cast on 2 sts, k25 sts from muzzle holder, cast on 2 sts, k17 sts from 2nd earflap holder, cast on 8 sts—80 sts. Join and pm, taking care not to twist sts on needle. Cont in pat sts as foll:
Rnd 1 P28, pm, k25, pm, p27.
Rnd 2 Knit. Rep rnds 1 and 2 (slipping markers every rnd) for 5"/12.5cm, end with rnd 1.

CROWN SHAPING
Change to dpns (dividing sts evenly between 4 needles) when there are too few sts on circular needle.
Dec rnd 1 *K8, k2tog; rep from * around—72 sts. Purl next rnd.
Dec rnd 2 *K7, k2tog; rep from * around—64 sts. Purl next rnd.
Dec rnd 3 *K6, k2tog; rep from * around—56 sts. Purl next rnd.

Gauge
20 sts and 42 rnds to 4"/10cm over garter st using size 7 (4.5mm) needle.
Take time to check gauge.

Dec rnd 4 *K5, k2tog; rep from * around—48 sts. Purl next rnd.
Dec rnd 5 *K4, k2tog; rep from * around—40 sts. Purl next rnd.
Dec rnd 6 *K3, k2tog; rep from * around—32 sts. Purl next rnd.
Dec rnd 7 *K2, k2tog; rep from * around—24 sts. Purl next rnd.
Dec rnd 8 *K1, k2tog; rep from * around—16 sts. Purl next rnd.
Dec rnd 9 [K2tog] 8 times—8 sts. Purl next rnd. Cut yarn, leaving an 8"/20.5cm tail and thread through rem sts. Pull tog tightly and secure end.

Eyes
(make two)
With dpns and A, cast on 24 sts. Working back and forth, knit 2 rows, purl one row.
Dec row 1 (RS) Sl 1, *k2tog, k1; rep from * to last 2 sts, end k2tog—16 sts. Purl next row.
Dec row 2 (RS) [K2tog] 8 times—8 sts. Purl next row.
Dec row 3 (RS) [K2tog] 4 times—4 sts. Purl next row.
Dec row 4 (RS) [K2tog] twice—2 sts.
Dec row 5 (WS) P2tog. Fasten off last st. Cut yarn, leaving a long tail for sewing.

PUPIL
With dpns and B, cast on 3 sts. Working back and forth, purl one row.
Inc row (RS) K1, (k1, yo, k1) in next st, k1—5 sts. Purl next row.
Dec row 1 (RS) K1, k3tog, k1—3 sts.
Dec row 2 (WS) P3tog. Fasten off last st. Cut yarn, leaving a long tail for sewing.

Nose
Beg at bottom edge, with dpns and B, cast on 3 sts. Work back and forth in St st for 6 rows.
Inc row 1 (RS) Sl 1, (k1, yo, k1) in next st, p1—5 sts. Purl next row.
Inc row 2 (RS) Sl 1, [k1, M1] twice, k1, p1—7 sts. Purl one row, knit one row, purl one row.
Dec row 1 (RS) Sl 1, ssk, k1, k2tog, p1—5 sts. Purl next row.
Dec row 2 (RS) Sl 1, k3tog, p1—3 sts. Bind off all sts purlwise.

Ears
(make 4)
With dpns and MC, cast on 24 sts. Working back and forth, knit 3 rows.
Dec row 1 (RS) Sl 1, *k2tog, k1; rep from * to last 2 sts, end k2tog—16 sts. Knit next row.
Dec row 2 (RS) [K2tog] 8 times—8 sts. Knit next row.
Dec row 3 (RS) [K2tog] 4 times—4 sts. Knit next row.
Dec row 4 (RS) [K2tog] twice—2 sts.
Dec row 5 (WS) K2tog. Fasten off last st. Cut yarn, leaving a long tail for sewing.

Finishing
MUZZLE
On center front of hat, measure 2½"/6.5cm up from last row of muzzle. Fold muzzle over to RS so top edge is even with 2½"/6.5cm measurement. Using A, whip stitch (see page 24) muzzle in place, easing in fullness so muzzle poufs out and adds dimension.

EYES
With RS of eyes facing, position eyes so bottom edges butt top edge of muzzle and outside edges butt first and last St sts. Using A, whipstitch in place. Sew on pupils.

NOSE
Using B, sew on nose as in photo.

EARS
For each ear, place 2 pieces tog with RS facing. Whipstitch tog along curved edge; turn RS out. Sew ears to each side of head so bottom edges are even with last row of earflaps. ■

Front

Back

Diagonal Stripes Hat

Get your twirl on in this obliquely striped topper. Cleverly knotted I-cords trim the band and sprout from the top, adding another dimension to this fun-loving hat.

DESIGNED BY JILL WRIGHT

INTERMEDIATE

Sizes
Instructions are written for one size.

Finished measurements
Circumference 18½"/47cm
Depth 7½"/19cm (excluding I-cords)

Materials
■ 1 3½oz/100g hank (each approx 220yd/201m) of Cascade Yarns *220 Wool Quatro* (Peruvian highland wool) in #5022 oceanside (A)

■ 1 3½oz/100g hank (each approx 220yd/201m) of Cascade Yarns *220 Wool Heathers* (Peruvian highland wool) in #2433 pacific (B)

■ One pair size 7 (4.5mm) needles *or size to obtain gauge*

■ Two size 7 (4.5mm) double-pointed needles (dpns) for I-cords

■ Bobbins (optional)

■ Stitch holder

Notes
1) When changing colors, pick up new color from under dropped color to prevent holes.
2) Do not carry colors across, use a separate strand (or bobbin) of color for each color section.

Hat
KNOTTED I-CORD TRIM
**With dpn and A, cast on 5 sts, leaving a long tail. Work in I-cord as foll:
*Next row (RS) With 2nd dpn, k5, do not turn. Slide sts back to beg of needle to work next row from RS; rep from * until I-cord measures 3"/7.5cm from beg. Turn.
Next row (WS) P5. Cut yarn, leaving a 36"/91.5cm tail. Place these 5 sts on straight needle ready for a RS row. Make another I-cord using B and place on needle**. Rep from ** to **, until 20

I-cords are on needle (10 A and 10 B). AT THE SAME TIME, cut yarn, leaving tail lengths as foll: 6yd/5.5m for 3rd cord, 9yd/8.25m for 4th cord and 12yd/11m for the 16 rem cords. Cont in St st as foll:
Beg chart pat
Row 1 (RS) Work 10-st rep 10 times. Cont to foll chart in this way to row 20, then rep rows 1–20 until piece measures 7"/17.5cm from beg (excluding I-cords), end on row 2 or 12.

CROWN SHAPING
Keeping to color changes as established, work as foll:
Row 1 (RS) *K3, SKP; rep from * to end—80 sts (each stripe is now 4 sts wide).
Row 2 Purl.
Row 3 *K2, SKP; rep from * to end—60 sts (each stripe is now 3 sts wide).
Row 4 Purl.

KNOTTED I-CORD FRINGE
Note There are 10 I-cords at top of hat. Each I-cord uses 3 sts from pairs of same-color stripes. Cont to keep color changes as established, work as foll:

First I-cord
Next row (RS) Place next 3 sts on holder, with dpn k next 3 sts, place next 3 sts on same st holder and hold to back of

Gauge
22 sts and 29 rows to 4"/10cm over chart pat using size 7 (4.5mm) needles. *Take time to check gauge.*

Diagonal Stripes Hat

work, using same dpn, k next st,
then k2tog—5 sts on dpn. **Work I-cord
for 8½"/21.5cm.
Next row (RS) [K2tog] twice, k1—3 sts.
Slide sts back to beg of needle to work
next row from RS.
Next row (RS) K3tog. Fasten off last st.
Weave in end.**

Second I-cord
Next row (RS) Place 6 sts on holder back
to LH needle, with dpn, k4, k2tog—5 sts
on dpn. Rep from ** to ** as for first
I-cord. Rep first and second I-cords 4
times more.

Finishing
Sew back seam. Make a single overhand
knot in each I-cord around bottom edge
of hat, making sure they all face in the
same direction. I-cords at top of hat can
be tied in different combinations to either
leave a hole for a ponytail or close up
the hole with one knot or a series of
smaller knots. Try a few variations to see
what you prefer. ■

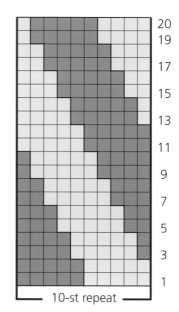

20
19
17
15
13
11
9
7
5
3
1

10-st repeat

Color Key

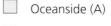

Oceanside (A)

Pacific (B)

220 Wool Quatro is made up of four
strands of different hues, plied
together for a multidimensional look.

Wave Scarf

Wade into tranquil waters with this beautiful sea-glass-hued scarf. A variegated yarn adds depth to a surprisingly simple ribbed scarf.

DESIGNED BY DEBBIE O'NEILL

INTERMEDIATE

Finished measurements
Approx 5½" x 68"/14cm x 172.5cm

Materials
- 2 3½oz/100g hanks (each approx 220yd/201m) of Cascade Yarns *220 Paints* (Peruvian highland wool) in #9848 aqua sol
- One pair size 7 (4.5mm) needles *or size to obtain gauge*

Notes
1) Chart shows RS rows only.
2) Work rows 1-4 on first rep of chart only, rep rows 5-84 for all subsequent reps.
3) First row of chart decreases number of sts to 45. These 45 sts are maintained except for rows 41 and 81, which decrease to 43 sts, then rows 43 and 83 increase back to 45 sts.

Increasing and decreasing in the pattern naturally creates a wavy silhouette.

Stitch glossary
M2 (make 2) Knit into front, back, then front of stitch.

Scarf
Cast on 47 sts.
Set-up row (WS) P1, *k1, p1; rep from * to end.
Beg chart pat
Row 1 (RS) Work to end of row - 45 sts.
Row 2 and all WS rows P1, *k1, p1; rep from * to end.
Cont to foll chart and work WS rows in this way to row 84, then rep rows 5-84 until piece measures 68"/172.5cm from beg, end with a RS row. Complete as per pattern.

Finishing
Block piece lightly to measurements. ■

Gauge
30 sts and 27 rows to 4"/10cm over k1, p1, rib using size 7 (4.5mm) needles.
Take time to check gauge.

Wave Scarf

Stitch Key

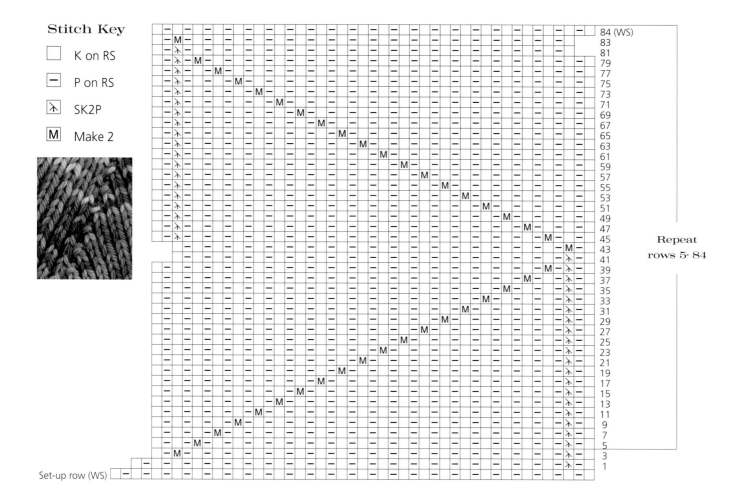

Set-up row (WS)

Repeat
rows 5-84

84 (WS)

Stitch Key

☐ K on RS

– P on RS

⅄ SK2P

M Make 2

---

*✳ **Quick Tip**
There are many ways to increase stitches in a knitting pattern.
The increase used here creates three stitches from one.*

12

Cables & Wraps Scarf

Cross the sands of time with this cabled and wrapped scarf that evokes ancient Egyptian motifs. Knit in a warm butterscotch color, it's the perfect accent for your fall wardrobe.

DESIGNED BY JACQUELINE VAN DILLEN

■■■■□□ EXPERIENCED

Finished measurements
Approx 7½" x 53"/19cm x 134.5cm (excluding fringe)

Materials
■ 2 3½oz/100g hanks (each approx 220yd/201m) of Cascade Yarns *220 Wool Heathers* (Peruvian highland wool) in #2437 kansas

■ One pair size 7 (4.5mm) needles *or size to obtain gauge*

■ Size H/8 (5mm) crochet hook (for fringe)

Stitch glossary
inc Work (k1, yo, k1) in st—2 sts increased.

Pattern stitch
(multiple of 18 sts plus 5)
Row 1 (RS) P1, *k1, inc in next st, k1, p2, k1 tbl, p2, k1, k3tog, k1, p2, k1 tbl, p2; rep from * once more, end k1, inc in next st, k1, p1.
Row 2 K1, p5, *k2, p1 tbl, k2, p3, k2, p1 tbl, k2, p5; rep from * once more, end k1.

Row 3 P1, *k2, inc in next st, k2, p2, k1 tbl, p2, sl 3 wyif, p2, k1 tbl, p2; rep from * once more, end k2, inc in next st, k2, p1.
Row 4 K1, p7, *k2, p1 tbl, k2, sl 3 wyib, k2, p1 tbl, k2, p7; rep from * once more, end k1.
Row 5 P1, *k7, p2, k1 tbl, p2, sl 3 wyif, p2, k1 tbl, p2; rep from * once more, end k7, p1.
Row 6 Rep row 4.

Gauge
22 sts and 26 rows to 4"/10cm over pat st using size 7 (4.5mm) needles.
Take time to check gauge.

Cables & Wraps Scarf

Row 7 P1, *k2, k3tog, k2, p2, k1 tbl, p2, sl 3 wyif, p2, k1 tbl, p2; rep from * once more, end k2, k3tog, k2, p1.
Row 8 Rep row 2.
Row 9 P1, *k1, k3tog, k1, p2, k1 tbl, p2, k1, inc in next st, k1, p2, k1 tbl, p2; rep from * once more, end k1, k3tog, k1, p1.
Row 10 K1, p3, *k2, p1 tbl, k2, p5, k2, p1 tbl, k2, p3; rep from * once more, end k1.
Row 11 P1, *sl 3 wyif, p2, k1 tbl, p2, k2, inc in st, k2, p2, k1 tbl, p2; rep from * once more, end sl 3 wyif, p1.
Row 12 K1, sl 3 wyib, *k2, p1 tbl, k2, p7, k2, p1 tbl, k2, sl 3 wyib; rep from * once more, end k1.
Row 13 P1, *sl 3 wyif, p2, k1 tbl, p2, k7, p2, k1 tbl, p2; rep from * once more, end sl 3 wyif, p1.
Row 14 Rep row 12.
Row 15 P1, *sl 3 wyif, p2, k1 tbl, p2, k2, k3tog, k2, p2, k1 tbl, p2; rep from * once more, end sl 3 wyif, p1.
Row 16 Rep row 10.
Rep rows 1–16 for pat st.

Scarf
Cast on 41 sts. Knit next 2 rows. Cont in pat st until piece measures 54"/137cm from beg, end with row 8 or 16. Knit next 2 rows. Bind off all sts knitwise.

Finishing
Block piece lightly to measurements.

FRINGE
Cut 8"/20.5cm lengths yarn. Using 5 strands for each fringe, attach 10 fringe evenly spaced across each end. Trim ends evenly. ■

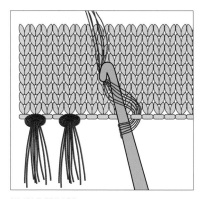

SIMPLE FRINGE
Cut yarn twice desired length plus extra for knotting. On wrong side, insert hook from front to back through piece and over folded yarn. Pull yarn through. Draw ends through and tighten. Trim yarn.

Quick Tip
Don't be intimidated by the intricate-looking stitch. By bringing the yarn to the front and back, a wrapped illusion is created.

Ribbed Wristers

Extra-long and snug-fitting, these ribbed gauntlets will keep hands of all sizes warm. They're knit in quick 2x2 ribbing and can easily be lengthened or shortened to suit the wearer's needs.

DESIGNED BY TANIS GRAY

EASY

Sizes
Instructions are written for size Small/Medium. Changes for Large are in parentheses.

Finished measurements
Hand circumference 4¾ (5½)"/12 (14)cm (unstretched)
Length 7½"/19cm

Materials
■ 1 3½oz/100g hank (each approx 220yd/201m) of Cascade Yarns *220 Wool* (Peruvian highland wool) in #7801 rouge red

■ One set (4) size 8 (5mm) double-pointed needles (dpns) *or size to obtain gauge*

■ Stitch holder

■ Stitch marker

Wristers (make 2)
With dpns, cast on 24 (28) sts and divide sts evenly over 3 needles. Join, taking care not to twist sts on needles, pm for beg of rnds. Work around in k2, p2 rib for 5"/12.5cm.
Next (thumbhole) rnd K2, p2, k2, place these 6 sts on holder, work in rib to end.
Next rnd Cast on 6 sts, work in rib to end. Cont in rib until piece measures 7½"/19cm from beg.
Bind off in rib pat.

THUMB
Divide 6 thumb sts over 2 needles.
Next rnd Join yarn and work in rib pat across sts, with 3rd needle, pick up and k 6 sts across cast-on sts of thumbhole—12 sts. Divide sts over 3 dpns. Join and pm for beg of rnds. Cont in rib pat for 7 rnds.
Bind off loosely in rib pat. ■

Gauge
20 sts and 24 rnds to 4"/10cm over rib pat using size 8 (5mm) dpns.
Take time to check gauge.

Zigzag Scarf

Densely knit in an opposites-attract relief pattern that uses only knits and purls, this simple scarf easily walks the line between fashion and function.

DESIGNED BY AMANDA BLAIR BROWN

Finished measurements

Approx 5" x 60"/12.5cm x 152.5cm

Materials

■ 1 3½oz/100g hank (each approx 220yd/201m) of Cascade Yarns *220 Wool Heathers* (Peruvian highland wool) in #8401 silver grey

■ One pair size 7 (4.5mm) needles *or size to obtain gauge*

Pattern stitch (over 32 sts)

Rows 1 and 2 Sl 1, [k5 tbl, p5 tbl] 3 times, k1.

Row 3 Sl 1, k4 tbl, [p5 tbl, k5 tbl] twice, p5 tbl, k1 tbl, k1.

Row 4 Sl 1, p1 tbl, [k5 tbl, p5 tbl] twice, k5 tbl, p4 tbl, k1.

Row 5 Sl 1, k3 tbl, [p5 tbl, k5 tbl] twice, p5 tbl, k2 tbl, k1.

Row 6 Sl 1, p2 tbl, [k5 tbl, p5 tbl] twice, k5 tbl, p3 tbl, k1.

Row 7 Sl 1, k2 tbl, [p5 tbl, k5 tbl] twice, p5 tbl, k3 tbl, k1.

Row 8 Sl 1, p3 tbl, [k5 tbl, p5 tbl] twice, k5 tbl, p2 tbl, k1.

Row 9 Sl 1, k1 tbl, [p5 tbl, k5 tbl] twice, p5 tbl, k4 tbl, k1.

Row 10 Sl 1, p4 tbl, [k5 tbl, p5 tbl] twice, k5 tbl, p1 tbl, k1.

Rows 11 and 12 Sl 1, [p5 tbl, k5 tbl] 3 times, k1.

Row 13 Sl 1, p4 tbl, [k5 tbl, p5 tbl] twice, k5 tbl, p1 tbl, k1.

Row 14 Sl 1, k1 tbl, [p5 tbl, k5 tbl] twice, p5 tbl, k4 tbl, k1.

Row 15 Sl 1, p3 tbl, [k5 tbl, p5 tbl] twice, k5 tbl, p2 tbl, k1.

Row 16 Sl 1, k2 tbl, [p5 tbl, k5 tbl] twice, p5 tbl, k3 tbl, k1.

Row 17 Sl 1, p2 tbl, [k5 tbl, p5 tbl] twice, k5 tbl, p3 tbl, k1.

Row 18 Sl 1, k3 tbl, [p5 tbl, k5 tbl] twice, p5 tbl, k2 tbl, k1.

Row 19 Sl 1, p1 tbl, [k5 tbl, p5 tbl] twice, k5 tbl, p4 tbl, k1.

Row 20 Sl 1, k4 tbl, [p5 tbl, k5 tbl] twice, p5 tbl, k1 tbl, k1.

Rows 21–40 Rep rows 1–20.

Rows 41 and 42 Sl 1, [k5 tbl, p5 tbl] 3 times, k1.

Rows 43 and 44 Sl 1, [p5 tbl, k5 tbl] 3 times, k1.

Row 45 Sl 1, k1 tbl, [p5 tbl, k5 tbl] twice, p5 tbl, k4 tbl, k1.

Row 46 Sl 1, p4 tbl, [k5 tbl, p5 tbl] twice, k5 tbl, p1 tbl, k1.

Row 47 Sl 1, k2 tbl, [p5 tbl, k5 tbl] twice, p5 tbl, k3 tbl, k1.

Row 48 Sl 1, p3 tbl, [k5 tbl, p5 tbl] twice, k5 tbl, p2 tbl, k1.

Row 49 Sl 1, k3 tbl, [p5 tbl, k5 tbl] twice, p5 tbl, k2 tbl, k1.

Row 50 Sl 1, p2 tbl, [k5 tbl, p5 tbl] twice, k5 tbl, p3 tbl, k1.

Row 51 Sl 1, k4 tbl, [p5 tbl, k5 tbl] twice, p5 tbl, k1 tbl, k1.

Row 52 Sl 1, p1 tbl, [k5 tbl, p5 tbl] twice, k5 tbl, p4 tbl, k1.

Rows 53 and 54 Sl 1, [k5 tbl, p5 tbl] 3 times, k1.

Row 55 Sl 1, p1 tbl, [k5 tbl, p5 tbl] twice, k5 tbl, p4 tbl, k1.

Row 56 Sl 1, k4 tbl, [p5 tbl, k5 tbl] twice, p5 tbl, k1 tbl, k1.

Row 57 Sl 1, p2 tbl, [k5 tbl, p5 tbl] twice, k5 tbl, p3 tbl, k1.

Row 58 Sl 1, k3 tbl, [p5 tbl, k5 tbl] twice, p5 tbl, k2 tbl, k1.

Row 59 Sl 1, p3 tbl, [k5 tbl, p5 tbl] twice, k5 tbl, p2 tbl, k1.

Row 60 Sl 1, k2 tbl, [p5 tbl, k5 tbl] twice, p5 tbl, k3 tbl, k1.

Row 61 Sl 1, p4 tbl, [k5 tbl, p5 tbl] twice, k5 tbl, p1 tbl, k1.

Row 62 Sl 1, k1 tbl, [p5 tbl, k5 tbl] twice, p5 tbl, k4 tbl, k1.

Rows 63–82 Rep rows 43–62.

Rows 83 and 84 Sl 1, [p5 tbl, k5 tbl] 3 times, k1.

Rep rows 1–84 for pat st.

Scarf

Cast on 32 sts. Rep rows 1–84 of pat st 4 times, then rows 1–83 once. Bind off foll row 84.

Finishing

Block piece lightly to measurements. ■

Gauge

25 sts and 28 rows to 4"/10cm over pat st using size 7 (4.5mm) needles. *Take time to check gauge.*

Striped & Bobbled Hat

Knit in sugary shades of superwash, this slouchy hat is a treat for any little girl who loves pink. The citrusy-green band keeps it from being overly sweet.

DESIGNED BY SUSAN ANDERSON

■□□□
BEGINNER

Sizes
Instructions are written for Child size Small/Medium. Changes for Large are in parentheses.

Finished measurements
Circumference
15¼ (16¾)"/ 38.5 (42.5)cm
Depth 10"/25.5cm

Materials
■ 1 3½oz/100g ball (each approx 220yd/201m) of Cascade Yarns *220 Superwash* (superwash wool) each in #839 medium rose (A), #886 citron (B) and #807 raspberry (C)

■ Size 7 (4.5mm) circular needle, 16"/40cm length *or size to obtain gauge*

■ One set (4) size 7 (4.5mm) double-pointed needles (dpns)

■ Stitch marker

Stitch glossary
Make bobble (MB) K1, p1, k1 in same st, making 3 sts from one; turn. P3, turn. K3, turn. P3, turn. K2tog, k1, pass first st over 2nd st.

Hat
With circular needle and A, cast on 80 (88) sts. Join and pm, taking care not to twist sts on needle. Change to B. Work in k1, p1 rib for 8 rnds. Change to C.
Rnd 1 Knit.
Rnd 2 *K3, MB; rep from * around.
Rnds 3–8 Knit. Change to A.
Rnds 9–16 Knit. Change to C.
Rnds 17–24 Rep rnds 1–8. Change to A.
Rnds 25–28 Knit.
Rnd (inc) 29 *K4, M1; rep from * around—100 (110) sts.
Rnds 30–32 Knit. Change to C.
Rnds 33–40 Rep rnds 1–8. Change to A.
Rnds 41–48 Knit. Change to B.
Rnd (inc) 49 *K5, M1; rep from * around—120 (132) sts.
Rnds 50–52 Knit. Change to A.
Rnds 53–56 Knit. Change to B.
Rnds 57–60 Knit. Change to A.

CROWN SHAPING
Change to dpns (dividing sts evenly over 3 needles) when there are too few sts on circular needle.
Rnd 1 *K4, k2tog; rep from * around—100 (110) sts.
Rnd 2 *K3, k2tog; rep from * around—80 (88) sts.
Rnds 3 and 4 Knit. Change to B.
Rnd 5 *K2, k2tog; rep from * around—60 (66) sts.
Rnd 6 *K1, k2tog; rep from * around—40 (44) sts.
Rnd 7 *K2tog; rep from * around—20 (22) sts.
Rnd 8 [K2tog] 10 (11) times—10 (11) sts.
Cut yarn, leaving an 8"/20.5cm tail and thread through rem sts. Pull tog tightly and secure end. ■

Gauge
21 sts and 28 rnds to 4"/10cm over St st using size 7 (4.5mm) circular needle. *Take time to check gauge.*

16 Ribbed Bonnet

Keep your coif covered with this take on a classic bonnet. Updated with pompoms and I-cord ties, it will make you feel like a modern-day pioneer girl.

DESIGNED BY CATHY CARRON

Sizes
Instructions are written for one size.

Finished measurements
Approx 8½" x 10"/21.5cm x 25.5cm

Materials
- 2 3½oz/100g hanks (each approx 220yd/201m) of Cascade Yarns *220 Wool Heathers* (Peruvian highland wool) in #9324 misty lilac heather
- Size 10 (6mm) circular needle, 24"/61cm length *or size to obtain gauge*
- One set (4) size 10 (6mm) double-pointed needles (dpns)
- Stitch marker
- Tapestry needle

Stitch glossary
Inc Knit into front and back of stitch.

Notes
1) Use a double strand of yarn throughout.
2) Hat is made from the top of the crown down.
3) Crown is worked in the rnd on dpns and sides are worked back and forth on circular needle.

Bonnet
CROWN
With dpns and 2 strands of yarn held tog, cast on 12 sts, leaving a long tail for sewing. Divide sts over 3 needles. Join, taking care not to twist sts on needles, pm for beg of rnds.
Rnd 1 Knit.
Rnd 2 [Inc] 12 times—24 sts.
Rnd 3 Knit.
Rnd 4 *K1, inc; rep from * around—36 sts.
Rnd 5 Knit.
Rnd 6 *Inc; rep from around—72 sts.
Rnd 7 Knit.
Rnd 8 Rep rnd 4—108 sts.
Rnd 9 [Inc] 3 times, k to end—111 sts.
Cont to work back and forth in rib pat on dpn as foll:

SIDES
Row 1 (RS) K3, *p3, k3; rep from * to end.
Row 2 P3, *k3, p3; rep from * to end. Rep rows 1 and 2 for rib pat. Work even for 6"/15cm, changing to circular needle after approx 2"/5cm, end with a WS row.
Next (dec) row K3tog tbl, *p3, k3tog tbl; rep from * to end—73 sts.

CASING
Cont in reverse St st as foll:

Row 1 (WS) Knit.
Row 2 Purl. Rep rows 1 and 2 twice more. Bind off all sts loosely knitwise.

Finishing
Thread beg tail of hat in tapestry needle. Weave tail around opening at top of crown. Pull tog tightly and secure end. Fold casing in half to WS and sew in place using a single strand of yarn.

I-CORD TIE
With dpn and 2 strands of yarn held tog, cast on 3 sts, leaving a long tail for sewing. Work in I-cord as foll:
*Next row (RS) With 2nd dpn, k3, do not turn. Slide sts back to beg of needle to work next row from RS; rep from * until I-cord measures 55"/139.5cm from beg. Cut yarn, leaving a 6"/15.5cm tail. Thread tail in tapestry needle, then thread through rem sts. Pull tog tightly and secure end. Thread beg tail in tapestry needle. Weave tail around opening at beg of I-cord. Pull tog tightly and secure end. Thread I-cord tie through casing. Make 2 pompoms 2½"/6.5cm in diameter. Sew pompoms to ends of I-cord ties. ■

Gauge
19 sts and 18 rows to 4"/10cm over k3, p3 rib using double strand of yarn and size 10 (6mm) needle. *Take time to check gauge.*

Plaid Mittens

You'll go mad for plaid with these tartan mittens. They're knit in Fair Isle and simple stripes, with the vertical stripes added last in duplicate stitching. Plaid has never been simpler!

DESIGNED BY HELEN SHARP

INTERMEDIATE

Sizes
Instructions are written for one size.

Finished measurements
Hand circumference 7½"/19cm
Length of cuff approx 3½"/9cm

Materials
■ 1 3½oz/100g hank (each approx 220yd/201m) of Cascade Yarns *220 Wool* (Peruvian highland wool) each in #8895 christmas red (MC), #8505 white (A), #8884 claret (B) and #7815 summer sky

■ One pair size 8 (5mm) needles *or size to obtain gauge*

■ One set (4) size 8 (5mm) double-pointed needles (dpns) *or size to obtain gauge*

■ Stitch holder

■ Stitch markers

Note
Mittens are worked back and forth on straight needles and thumbs are worked in the rnd on dpns.

Stitch Glossary
M1R (make 1 right) Insert LH needle from *back* to *front* into the strand between last st worked and the next st on the LH needle. Knit into the front loop to twist the st.
M1L (make 1 left) Insert LH needle from *front to back* into the strand between last st worked and the next st on the LH needle. Knit into the back loop to twist the st.

Mittens (make 2)
CUFF
With straight needles and MC, cast on 34 sts. Cont in rib pat as foll:
Row 1 (RS) [K2, p2] 4 times, pm, k2, pm, [p2, k2] 4 times.
Row 2 P2, *k2, p2; rep from * to end.
Row 3 K2, *p2, k2; rep from * to end.
Rep rows 2 and 3 until piece measures 3½"/9cm from beg, end with a WS row. Cont in St st as foll:
Beg chart pat
Beg chart on row 1 and work even through row 6.

THUMB GUSSET
Row 7 (RS) With C, k to first marker, slip marker, M1R, k2, M1L, slip marker, k to end—36 sts. Cont to foll chart in this way through row 18, working incs as shown—46 sts.
Row 19 (RS) With C, k to first marker, drop marker, place 14 thumb sts on scrap yarn, drop 2nd marker, k to end—32 sts.

Cont to work to top of chart, dec top of mitten as shown—12 sts. Place sts on holder.

THUMB
Place 14 sts on scrap yarn evenly over 3 needles. Join C, leaving a long tail for sewing and pick up and k 2 sts at base of thumb, k around to end—16 sts. Pm for beg of rnds. Knit next 4 rnds. Change to MC. Knit next rnd.

TOP SHAPING
Dec rnd 1 Ssk, k4, k2tog, ssk, k4, k2tog—12 sts. Knit next rnd.
Dec rnd 2 Ssk, k2, k2tog, ssk, k2, k2tog—8 sts. Knit next rnd.
Dec rnd 3 [Ssk, k2tog] twice—4 sts.
Cut yarn, leaving a 6"/15cm tail and thread through rem sts. Pull tog tightly and secure end. Use yarn tail at base of thumb to close up any gaps between thumb and hand.

Finishing
Referring to chart, use C to embroider duplicate stitches (see page 48). Following the same pat, cont duplicate stitches up each side of thumbs. Use MC to sew side seam. Using MC, graft sts tog at top of each mitten using Kitchener st or 3-needle bind-off. ■

Gauge
18 sts and 26 rows to 4"/10cm over St st using larger needles. *Take time to check gauge.*

Plaid Mittens

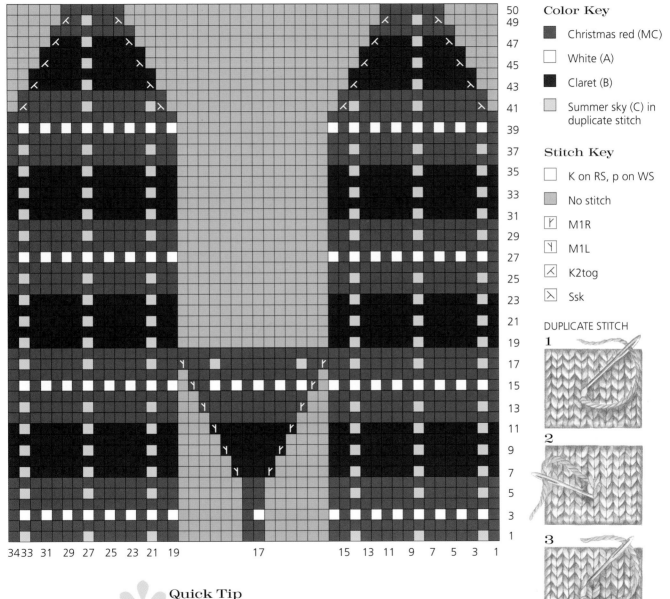

Color Key

- ■ Christmas red (MC)
- □ White (A)
- ■ Claret (B)
- ▨ Summer sky (C) in duplicate stitch

Stitch Key

- □ K on RS, p on WS
- ▨ No stitch
- ⼁ M1R
- ⼁ M1L
- ⼂ K2tog
- ⼁ Ssk

DUPLICATE STITCH

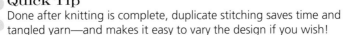

Quick Tip
Done after knitting is complete, duplicate stitching saves time and tangled yarn—and makes it easy to vary the design if you wish!

Striped Graduated Scarf

Knit in tweed stitch and three shades of gray and black, this tapered scarf points the way to the perfect present. As fun to wear as it is to knit, it will satisfy even the most persnickety.

DESIGNED BY JEAN SUZUKI

EXPERIENCED

Finished measurements
Approx 8½" (at widest point) x
59"/21.5cm x 150cm

Materials
■ 1 3½oz/100g hank (each approx
220yd/201m) of Cascade Yarns
220 Wool (Peruvian highland wool) each
in #8555 black (A), #9473 gris (B) and
#8509 grey (C)

■ Size 9 (5.5mm) circular needle,
32"/81cm length *or size to obtain gauge*

Notes
1) Scarf is knit horizontally from long
edge to opposite long edge and uses
short-row shaping to create tapered ends.
2) Circular needle is used to
accommodate the large number of sts.
Do not join, but work back and forth
in rows.

Short-row wrapping
(wrap and turn—w&t)
RIGHT SIDE
1) Work specified number of sts or work
to specified st.
2) Wyib, slip next st knitwise onto RH
needle.
3) Wyif, slip st back onto LH needle
(one wrapped st), turn to WS and work
back specified number of sts or work
to specified st.

4) When you have completed short rows,
k to wrapped st. Insert RH needle under
the wrap and place it on LH needle. Knit
it tog with next stitch on LH needle.

WRONG SIDE
1) Work specified number of sts or
work to specified st.
2) Wyif, slip next st knitwise onto RH
needle.
3) Wyib, slip st back onto LH needle
(one wrapped st), turn to RS and work
back specified number of sts or work to
specified st..
4) When you have completed short rows,
purl to wrapped st. Insert RH needle
under the wrap and place it on LH
needle. Purl it tog with next stitch on
LH needle.

Tweed stitch
Row 1 (RS) K1, *k1, sl 1 purlwise wyif,
rep from *, end last rep k1.
Row 2 Purl.
Row 3 K1, *sl 1 purlwise wyif, k1;
rep from * to end.
Row 4 Purl.
Rep rows 1–4 for tweed st.

Gauge
16 sts and 28 rows to 4"/10cm over tweed st using size 9 (5.5mm) needle.
Take time to check gauge.

Striped Graduated Scarf

18

Scarf

STRIPE I

With A, loosely cast on 251 sts.

Next row (RS) Work row 1 of tweed st to last 6 sts, w&t.

Next row Work row 2 of tweed st to last 6 sts, w&t. **Note** To maintain tweed st pat, take care that slip sts alternate from one RS row to another. Working even, work rows 3 and 4 of tweed st.

*Next row (RS) Work row 1 of tweed st to within 6 sts of last wrapped st, w&t.

Next row Work row 2 of tweed st to within 6 sts of last wrapped st, w&t. Working even, work rows 3 and 4 of tweed st*. Rep from * to * 3 times more.

STRIPE II

*Change to B.

Next row (RS) With B, work row 1 of tweed st to within 6 sts of last wrapped st, w&t.

Next row With B, work row 2 of tweed st to within 6 sts of last wrapped st, w&t. Change to A. Working even, work rows 3 and 4 of tweed st*. Rep from * to * twice more.

STRIPE III

With B, work as foll:

*Next row (RS) Work row 1 of tweed st to within 6 sts of last wrapped st, w&t.

Next row Work row 2 of tweed st to within 6 sts of last wrapped st, w&t. Working even, work rows 3 and 4 of tweed st*. Rep from * to * once more, then work first 2 rows once more.

STRIPE IV

*Change to C.

Next row (RS) With C, work row 3 of tweed st to within 6 sts of last wrapped st, w&t.

Next row With C, work row 4 of tweed st to within 6 sts of last wrapped st, w&t. Change to B. Working even, work rows 1 and 2 of tweed st*. Rep from * to * twice more, then work first 2 rows once more.

STRIPE V

With C, work as foll:

*Next row (RS) Work row 1 of tweed st to within 6 sts of last wrapped st, w&t.

Next row Work row 2 of tweed st to within 6 sts of last wrapped st, w&t. Working even, work rows 3 and 4 of tweed st*. Rep from * to * once more.

Pick up short rows

Next row (RS) With C, k to first wrapped st. Foll step 4 of RS short-row wrapping, pick up and k wraps and k sts to top of stripe IV. Change to B and cont in the same way to top of stripe I.

Change to A and cont in the same way to end. Turn.

Next row With A, bind off all sts purlwise to first wrapped st. Foll step 4 of WS short-row wrapping, pick up and p wraps and p sts. AT THE SAME TIME, bind off sts purlwise as you go.

Finishing

Block piece lightly to measurements. ■

Quick Tip

This scarf is a great stash-buster! Mix and match your leftover bits of 220 to customize a palette.

Twisted Toque

Shake things up in this twisted topper. With deep ribbing and a sassy spiral-shaped body, this hat is sure to turn heads.

DESIGNED BY HELEN SHARP

Sizes
Instructions are written for one size.

Finished measurements
Circumference 21"/53.5cm
Depth 10½"/26.5cm

Materials
■ 1 3½oz/100g hank (each approx 220yd/201m) of Cascade Yarns *220 Wool Heathers* (Peruvian highland wool) in #2425 provence

■ Size 7 (4.5mm) circular needle, 16"/40cm length *or size to obtain gauge*

■ One set (4) size 7 (4.5mm) double-pointed needles (dpns)

■ Stitch marker

Hat
With circular needle, cast on 96 sts. Join and pm, taking care not to twist sts on needle. Work in k2, p2 rib for 3½"/9cm. Cont in twisted pat st as foll:
Rnd 1 *K6, k2tog, [p1, k1] twice, M1; rep * around.
Rnd 2 *K6, k2tog, [k1, p1] twice, M1; rep * around. Rep rnds 1 and 2 until piece measures 8½"/21.5cm from beg, end with rnd 2.

CROWN SHAPING
Change to dpns (dividing sts evenly between 3 needles) when there are too few sts on circular needle.
Dec rnd 1 *K6, k2tog, [p1, k1] twice; rep from * around—88 sts.
Dec rnd 2 *K6, k2tog, k1, p1, k1; rep from * around—80 sts.
Dec rnd 3 *K6, k2tog, p1, k1; rep from * around—72 sts.
Dec rnd 4 *K6, k2tog, k1; rep from * around—64 sts.
Dec rnd 5 *K6, k2tog; rep from * around—56 sts.

Dec rnd 6 *K2tog, k5; rep from * around—48 sts.
Dec rnd 7 *K2tog, k4; rep from * around—40 sts.
Dec rnd 8 *K2tog, k3; rep from * around—32 sts.
Dec rnd 9 *K2tog, k2; rep from * around—24 sts.
Dec rnd 10 *K2tog, k1; rep from * around—16 sts.
Dec rnd 11 [K2tog] 8 times—8 sts.
Cut yarn, leaving an 8"/20.5cm tail and thread through rem sts. Pull tog tightly and secure end. ■

Gauge
18 sts and 28 rnds to 4"/10cm over twisted pat st using size 7 (4.5mm) circular needle. *Take time to check gauge.*

Textured Triple-Stripe Scarf

You'll look smarter right away in this academic-inspired scarf, perfect for any home game.
Knit it in your team's colors to stand out in the crowd.

DESIGNED BY CATHY CARRON

EASY

Finished measurements
Approx 9½" x 70"/24cm x 178cm

Materials
■ 1 3½oz/100g hank (each approx 220yd/201m) of Cascade Yarns *220 Wool* (Peruvian highland wool) each in #7818 blue velvet (A) and #8894 christmas green (B)

■ Size 7 (4.5mm) circular needle, 29"/74cm length *or size to obtain gauge*

■ Stitch markers

Notes
1) Scarf is knit horizontally from one long edge to opposite long edge.
2) Circular needle is used to accommodate the large number of sts. Do not join, but work back and forth in rows.

Double moss stitch
(multiple of 4 sts plus 2)
Rows 1 and 2 *K2, p2; rep from * to end.
Rows 3 and 4 *P2, k2; rep from * to end.
Rep rows 1–4 for double moss st.

Seed stitch
(over an even number of sts)
Row 1 (RS) *K1, p1; rep from * to end.
Row 2 K the purl sts and p the knit sts.
Rep row 2 for seed st.

Scarf
With A, cast on 310 sts. Work as foll:
Rows 1–20 Work in double moss st.
Row 21 (RS) Knit. Change to B.
Row 22 Purl.
Rows 23–30 Work in seed st.

Row 31 Work in seed st over first 10 sts, pm, k to last 10 sts, pm, work in seed st to end.
Row 32 Work in seed st over first 10 sts, sl marker, p to last 10 sts, sl marker, work in seed st to end.
Rows 33–44 Rep rows 33 and 34 six times more, dropping markers on last row.
Rows 45–52 Work in seed st.
Row 53 Knit. Change to A.
Row 54 Purl.
Rows 55–74 Work in double moss st. Bind off all sts knitwise.

Finishing
Block piece lightly to measurements. ■

Gauge
18 sts and 32 rows to 4"/10cm over double moss st using size 7 (4.5mm) needle.
Take time to check gauge.

Birdcage Mittens

Watch your mitten knitting soar to new heights with these enchanting bird mittens. Using two shades and advanced techniques, these mitts are a great way to step up your Fair Isle skills.

DESIGNED BY ELLI STUBENRAUCH

EXPERIENCED

Sizes
Instructions are written for one size.

Finished measurements
Hand circumference 8"/20.5cm
Length of cuff approx 2¼"/5.5cm

Materials
■ 1 3½oz/100g hank (each approx 220yd/201m) of Cascade Yarns *220 Wool Heathers* (Peruvian highland wool) each in #2440 vinci (A) and #9489 red wine heather (B)

■ Contrasting heavy worsted-weight yarn (waste yarn)

■ One set (5) each size 4 and 5 (3.5 and 3.75mm) double-pointed needles (dpns) *or size to obtain gauge*

■ Stitch marker

Note
To work in the rnd, always read charts from right to left.

Stitch glossary
kfb Knit in front and back of st—1 st increased.

M1R (make 1 right) Insert left needle from *back* to *front* into the horizontal strand between the last st worked and the next st on left needle. Using color indicated on chart, knit this strand through the front loop to twist the st.
M1L (make 1 left) Insert left needle from *front* to *back* into the horizontal strand between the last st worked and the next st on left needle. Using color indicated on chart, knit this strand through the back loop to twist the st.

Corrugated rib
(multiple of 2 sts)
Rnd 1 *K1 with A, p1 with B; rep from * around.
Rep rnd 1 for corrugated rib.

Left mitten
CUFF
With smaller dpns and A, cast on 44 sts. Divide sts over 4 needles (11 sts on each). Join, taking care not to twist sts on needles, pm for beg of rnds. Cont in corrugated rib for 14 rnds. Change to larger dpns.
Next (inc) rnd With A (k8, kfb, k9, kfb, k4), [k1 with B, k1 with A] 4 times, kfb with B, k1 with A, [k1 B, k1 A] 4 times, kfb with B, k1 with A, k1 with B—48 sts. Cont in St st as foll:

Beg chart pat I
Beg chart on rnd 1 and work even through rnd 4.

THUMB GUSSET
Rnd 5 With A, M1R, k1, M1L, work to end of rnd—50 sts. Cont to foll chart in this way through rnd 23, working inc as shown—68 sts.
Rnd 24 Place 20 thumb sts on scrap yarn—48 sts. Cont to work to top of chart, dec top of mitten as shown—16 sts. Cut A, leaving a 12"/30.5cm tail. Place 8 sts from front on one needle and 8 sts from back on a 2nd needle. Graft sts tog using Kitchener st or 3-needle bind-off.

THUMB
Place 20 sts on scrap yarn evenly over 4 needles (5 sts on each). Pm for beg of rnds. Rejoin A, leaving a long tail for sewing.
Beg chart II
Beg chart on rnd 1 and work to top of of chart, inc and dec as shown—8 sts. Cut B leaving a 6"/15cm tail. Thread tail in tapestry needle, then thread through rem sts. Pull tog tightly and secure end.

Gauge
24 sts and 26 rnds to 4"/10cm over chart pat using larger dpns (after blocking).
Take time to check gauge.

Birdcage Mittens

Chart I

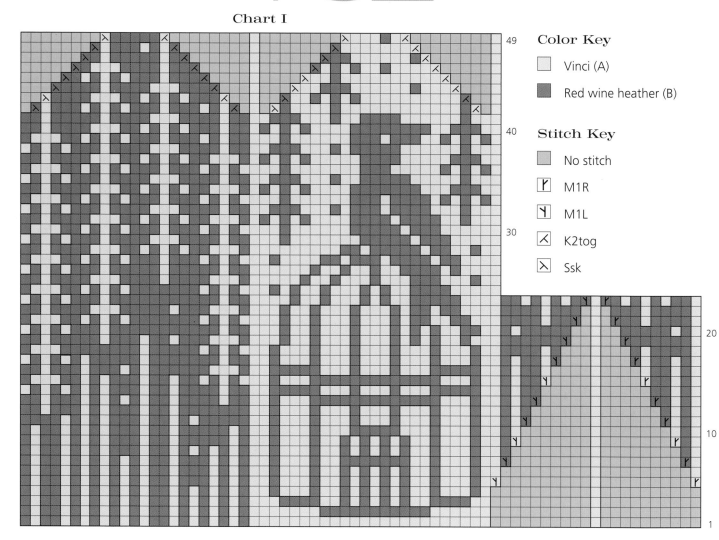

Color Key

- ☐ Vinci (A)
- ■ Red wine heather (B)

Stitch Key

- ☐ No stitch
- Ｒ M1R
- Ｌ M1L
- ⟋ K2tog
- ⟍ Ssk

Right mitten

CUFF

Work as for left mitten to inc rnd.

Next (inc) rnd K1 with A, k1 with B, k1 with A, kfb with B, [k1 with A, k1 with B] 4 times, k1 with A, kfb with B, [k1 with A, k1 with B] 4 times, with A (k4, kfb, k9, kfb, k7)—48 sts.

Cont to work as for left mitten, foll chart III for hand and chart II for thumb.

Finishing

For each mitten, use A tail to sew gap between thumb and hand closed. Block pieces to measurements. ■

58

Chart III

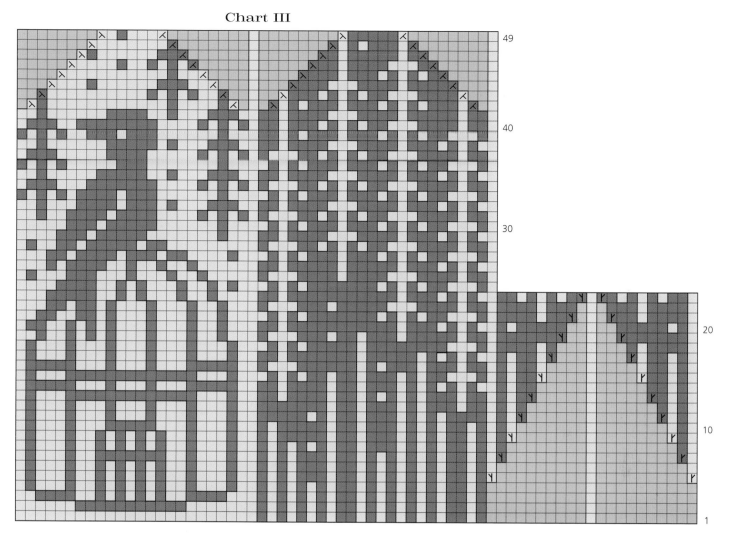

Chart II

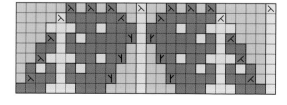

Quick Tip

Make sure you block your colorwork! Blocking evens out your work and is the finishing touch for any handknit.

59

Bobbles & Cables Cap

Knit in a beautiful amethyst heather, this cozy hat is no shrinking violet. The cables flow naturally from the ribbed band, and paired bobbles add extra texture.

DESIGNED BY SUVI SIMOLA

Sizes
Instructions are written for one size.

Finished measurements
Circumference 21"/53.5cm (slightly stretched)
Depth 7½"/19cm

Materials
■ 1 3½oz/100g hank (each approx 220yd/201m) of Cascade Yarns *220 Wool Heathers* (Peruvian highland wool) in #9453 amethyst heather

■ Sizes 6 and 7 (4 and 4.5mm) circular needles, 16"/40cm length *or size to obtain gauge*

■ One set (5) size 7 (4.5mm) double-pointed needles (dpns)

■ Cable needle (cn)

■ Stitch marker

Note
To work in the rnd, always read chart from right to left.

Stitch glossary
6-st RPC Sl 3 sts to cn and hold to *back*, k3, p3 from cn.
6-st LPC Sl 3 sts to cn and hold to *front*, p3, k3 from cn.
Make bobble [K1, p1] twice in same st, making 4 sts from one; then pass the 3rd, 2nd and first sts over the last st made.

M1 p-st With the needle tip, lift the strand between the last st worked and the next st on the LH needle and purl it.
M1R (make 1 right) Insert LH needle from *back* to *front* into the strand between last st worked and the next st on the LH needle. Knit into the front loop to twist the st.
M1L (make 1 left) Insert LH needle from *front* to *back* into the strand between last st worked and the next st on the LH needle. Knit into the back loop to twist the st.

Hat
With smaller circular needle, cast on 96 sts. Join and pm, taking care not to twist sts on needle. Cont in rib pat as foll:
Rnd 1 P1, *k2, p2; rep from *, end last rep p1 (instead of p2). Rep this rnd 8 times more.
Set-up rnd *P1, k2, M1L, p2, M1 p-st, p2, M1 p-st, p2, M1R, k2, p1; rep from * around—128 sts. Change to larger circular needle.

Gauge
20 sts and 28 rnds to 4"/10cm over St st using larger circular needle.
Take time to check gauge.

Bobbles & Cables Cap

Beg chart pat
Rnd 1 Work 16-st rep 8 times. Cont to foll chart in this way to rnd 24, then rep rnds 1–8 once more.

CROWN SHAPING
Change to dpns (dividing sts evenly between 4 needles) when there are too few sts on circular needle.
Rnd 1 *P1, k2, ssk, p6, k2tog, k2, p1; rep from * around—112 sts.
Rnd 2 and 4 K the knit sts and p the purl sts.
Rnd 3 *P1, k2, ssk, p4, k2tog, k2, p1; rep from * around—96 sts.
Rnd 5 *P1, k2, ssk, p2, k2tog, k2, p1; rep from * around—80 sts.
Rnd 6 *P1, k2, ssk, k2tog, k2, p1; rep from * around—64 sts.
Rnd 7 *P1, k2, ssk, k2, p1; rep from * around—56 sts.
Rnd 8 *P1, k2, ssk, k1, p1; rep from * around—48 sts.
Rnd 9 *P1, k2 ssk, p1; rep from * around—40 sts.
Rnd 10 *P1, k2, ssk; rep from * around—32 sts. Drop marker. Slip the last st from last rnd to LH needle, pm for new beg of rnd.
Rnd 11 *Ssk, k2; rep from * around—24 sts.
Rnd 12 *Ssk, k1; rep from * around—16 sts.
Rnd 13 [Ssk] 8 times—8 sts.
Cut yarn, leaving an 8"/20.5cm tail and thread through rem sts. Pull tog tightly and secure end. ■

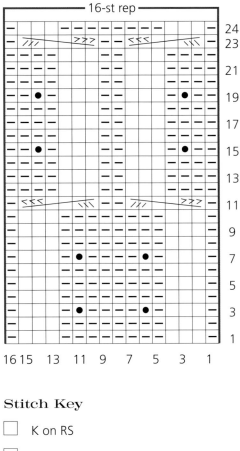

16 15   13   11   9   7   5   3   1

Stitch Key

☐ K on RS

— P on RS

● Make bobble

 6-st RPC

6-st LPC

 Quick Tip
If this is your first foray into knitting cables, practice first on a swatch to get the hang of it.

Smocked Fingerless Mitts

These skinny gauntlets are knit in two cable patterns that simulate smocking. Buttons, extra texture and a gorgeous berry-colored yarn make them dramatic adornments for a winter's evening.

DESIGNED BY TONIA BARRY

Sizes
Instructions are written for one size.

Finished measurements
Hand circumference 6¼"/16cm
Length of cuff approx 3"/7.5cm

Materials
■ 1 3½oz/100g hank (each approx 220yd/201m) of Cascade Yarns *220 Wool* (Peruvian highland wool) in #8909 raspberry
■ Contrasting heavy worsted-weight yarn (waste yarn)
■ One set (5) size 7 (4.5mm) double-pointed needles (dpns) *or size to obtain gauge*
■ Cable needle (cn)
■ Stitch markers
■ Ten ½"/12mm buttons

Note
To work in the rnd, always read charts from right to left.

Stitch glossary
RT (right twist) Skip next st on LH needle, k 2nd st in front of skipped st, then k skipped st, sl both sts from LH needle.
LT (left twist) With RH needle behind LH needle, skip next st on LH needle; knit 2nd st tbl, then knit skipped st in front lp, sl both sts from LH needle.
Wrap 2 sts twice Sl 2 sts to cn, with yarn in back, wrap yarn twice around these 2 sts, then k 2 from cn.

Gauge
25 sts and 30 rnds to 4"/10 cm over chart pat I using size 7 (4.5mm) dpns.
Take time to check gauge.

Smocked Fingerless Mitts

23

Left wrister

CUFF

With dpns, cast on 40 sts. Divide sts over 4 needles (10 sts on each). Join, taking care not to twist sts on needles, pm for beg of rnds. Cont in rib pat as foll:

Rnds 1 and 2 P1, *k2, p2; rep from * around, end k2, p1.

Beg chart pat I

Rnd 1 Work 8-st rep 5 times. Cont to foll chart in this way through rnd 16.

Rnd 17 K first st, rep sts 2–9 four times, then work sts 2–7 once, drop rnd marker, sl last st of this rnd and first st of next rnd to cn, wrap 2 sts twice, k1 from cn, pm, then place 2nd st on cn back to LH needle. Cont to foll chart to rnd 21.

Beg chart II

Rnd 1 Rep sts 1–4 three times, work sts 5–12 once, then rep sts 1–4 five times. Cont to foll chart in this way to rnd 8, then rep rnds 1–8 three times more. Cont to foll chart as foll:

THUMB PLACEMENT

Rnd 1 Work sts 1–4 three times, work sts 5–12 once, then rep sts 1–4 twice, work sts 1–4 twice onto waste yarn, sl these 8 sts back to LH needle, then with working yarn, work sts 1–4 twice more. Cont to foll chart to rnd 8, then rep rnds 1–8 once more, then rnds

1–4 once. Work in k2, p2 rib for 2 rnds. Bind off in rib.

THUMB

Remove waste yarn and place 16 live sts on dpns as foll: 8 sts below thumb opening on needle 1 and 8 sts above opening on needle 3. Place last 2 sts on needle one and first 3 sts on needle three onto needle two. Join yarn, leaving a long tail for sewing.

Beg chart III

Rnd 1 Rep sts 1–4 four times. Join and pm for beg of rnds. Cont to foll chart in this way to rnd 11. Bind off in pat st. Use yarn tail at base of thumb to close up gap between thumb and hand.

Finishing

On purl section, place markers for 5 buttons, with the first ¾"/2cm from beg of section, the last 1½"/4cm from top edge and the others evenly spaced between. Sew on buttons.

Right wrister

Work as for left wrister to chart II.

Beg chart II

Rnd 1 Work sts 1–8 once, then rep sts 9–12 eight times. Cont to foll chart in this way to rnd 8, then rep rnds 1–8 three times more. Cont to foll chart as foll:

THUMB PLACEMENT

Rnd 1 Work sts 1–8, then rep sts 9–12 three times, work sts 9–12 twice onto waste yarn, sl these 8 sts back to LH needle, then with working yarn, work sts 9–12 twice again, then rep sts 9–12 three times more. Cont to foll chart to rnd 8, then rep rnds 1–8 once more, then rnds 1–4 once. Work in k2, p2 rib for 2 rnds. Bind off in rib.

THUMB

Work as for left wrister. ■

Stitch Key

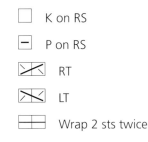

☐	K on RS
⊟	P on RS
⧅	RT
⧄	LT
⊞	Wrap 2 sts twice

Chart I

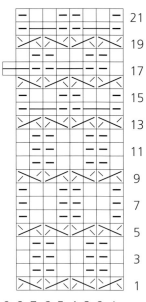

21
19
17
15
13
11
9
7
5
3
1

9 8 7 6 5 4 3 2 1

Chart II

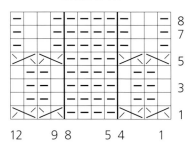

8
7
5
3
1

12   9 8   5 4   1

Chart III

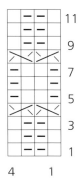

11
9
7
5
3
1

4   1

24

Mitered Scarf

This elegant scarf celebrates variegated yarns and clever construction. Knit using three colorways, it is a rich mosaic of vibrant blues and greens.

DESIGNED BY AMY POLCYN

INTERMEDIATE

Finished measurements
Approx 7¼" x 62"/18.5cm x 157.5cm

Materials
■ 1 3½oz/100g hank (each approx 220yd/201m) of Cascade Yarns *220 Paints* (Peruvian highland wool) each in #9862 tropical seas (A), #9863 spring meadows (B) and #9865 lucky clover (C)

■ One pair size 8 (5mm) needles *or size to obtain gauge*

Note
Mitered squares are worked in a stripe pat and mitered side triangles are worked in single colors.

Stripe pattern
Working in garter st, *work 2 rows A, 2 rows B, 2 rows C; rep from * (6 rows) for stripe pat.

Scarf
MITERED SQUARES (MAKE 8)
With A, cast on 51 sts.
Row 1(RS) Sl 1, knit to end.
Row 2 Sl 1, k23, S2KP, knit to end—49 sts. Change to B.
Row 3 Sl 1, knit to end.
Row 4 Sl 1, k22, S2KP, knit to end—47 sts. Change to C.

Row 5 Sl 1, knit to end.
Row 6 Sl 1, k21, S2KP, knit to end—45 sts. Change to A.
Row 7 Sl 1, knit to end.
Row 8 Sl 1, k20, S2KP, knit to end—43 sts. Change to B.
Row 9 Sl 1, knit to end.
Row 10 Sl 1, k19, S2KP, knit to end—41 sts. Change to C.
Row 11 Sl 1, knit to end.
Row 12 Sl 1, k18, S2KP, knit to end—39 sts. Change to A. Cont to work 1 st less before dec every WS row until 3 sts rem, end with a WS row. AT THE SAME TIME, cont to work in stripe pat as established.
Next row (RS) K3tog. Fasten off last st.

MITERED SIDE TRIANGLES
Referring to assembly diagram and direction of work, place first 2 squares tog with corners touching and RS facing. With RS facing and appropriate color, pick up and k 25 sts along side edge of first square (1 st per slipped st along edge), 1 st at tip where squares meet, then pick up and k 25 sts along side of second square—51 sts.

Gauge
20 sts and 40 rows to 4"/10cm over garter st size 8 (5mm) needles.
Take time to check gauge.

Mitered Scarf

Row 1 (WS) Sl 1, ssk, k21, S2KP, k to last 3 sts, k2tog, k1—47 sts.

Row 2 and all RS rows Sl 1, knit to end.

Row 3 Sl 1, ssk, k19, S2KP, k to last 3 sts, k2tog, k1—43 sts.

Row 5 Sl 1, ssk, k17, S2KP, k to last 3 sts, k2tog, k1—39 sts.

Row 7 Sl 1, ssk, k15, S2KP, k to last 3 sts, k2tog, k1—35 sts.

Row 9 Sl 1, ssk, k13, S2KP, k to last 3 sts, k2tog, k1—31 sts.

Row 11 Sl 1, ssk, k11, S2KP, k to last 3 sts, k2tog, k1—27 sts.

Row 13 Sl 1, ssk, k9, S2KP, k to last 3 sts, k2tog, k1—23 sts. Cont to work 2 sts less before S2KP every WS row until 3 sts rem, end with a WS row.

Next row (RS) K3tog. Fasten off last st. Work mitered side triangle along opposite side edges of mitered squares. Working in the same manner, cont to add a mitered square, then work mitered side triangles foll assembly diagram for direction of work and color placement.

Finishing

Block piece lightly to measurements. ◼

Assembly Diagram

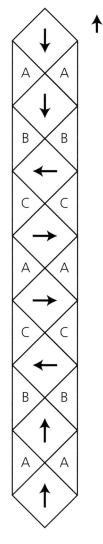

↑ = Direction of knitting

Ribbed Keyhole Scarf

Lay the foundation for a chic look with this simple neck wrap. Form follows function in a scarf designed to stay out of your way while keeping you toasty.

DESIGNED BY ANGELA JUERGENS

EASY

Finished measurements
Approx 9" x 38"/23cm x 96.5cm

Materials
■ 2 3½oz/100g hanks (each approx 220yd/201m) of Cascade Yarns *220 Wool Quatro* (Peruvian highland wool) in #5018 summerdaze

■ One pair size (4.5mm) needles *or size to obtain gauge*

Scarf
Cast on 78 sts. Cont in rib pat as foll:
Row 1 (RS) K6, *p6, k6; rep from * to end.
Row 2 P6, *k6, p6; rep from * to end.
Rep rows 1 and 2 until piece measures 5½"/14cm from beg, end with row 1.
Next (dec) row (WS) P6, *k4, k2tog, p6; rep from to end—72 sts.
Row 3 (RS) K6, *p5, k6; rep from * to end
Row 4 P6, *k5, p6; rep from * to end.
Rep rows 3 and 4 until piece measures 8½"/21.5cm from beg, end with row 3.

Next (dec) row (WS) P4, p2tog, *k5, p4, p2tog; rep from * to end—65 sts.
Row 5 (RS) K5, *p5, k5; rep from * to end.
Row 6 P5, *k5, p5; rep from * to end.
Rep rows 5 and 6 until piece measures 10½"/26.5cm from beg, end with row 5.
Next (dec) row (WS) P5, *k2tog, k3, p5; rep from * to end—59 sts.
Row 7 (RS) K5, *p4, k5; rep from * to end.

Gauge
20 sts and 28 rows to 4"/10cm over St st using size 7 (4.5mm) needles.
Take time to check gauge.

Ribbed Keyhole Scarf

Yarn Smarts

If you want to waterproof your knits, simply soak your project in two parts water and one part lanolin. Let dry and voilà!

Row 8 P5, *k4, p5; rep from * to end. Rep rows 7 and 8 until piece measures 13"/33cm from beg, end with row 7.

Next (dec) row (WS) P3, p2tog, *k4, p2tog, p3; rep from * to end—52 sts.

Row 9 (RS) K4, *p4, k4; rep from * to end.

Row 10 P4, *k4, p4; rep from * to end. Rep rows 9 and 10 until piece measures 24½"/62cm from beg, end with row 9.

Next (inc) row (WS) P2,m1 p-st, p2, *k4, p2,m1 p-st, p2; rep from * to end—59 sts.

Row 11 (RS) K5, *p4, k5; rep from * to end.

Row 12 P5, *k4, p5; rep from * to end. Rep rows 11 and 12 until piece measures 26½"/67.5cm from beg, end with row 11.

Next (inc) row (WS) P5, *k2, M1, k2, p5; rep from * to end—65 sts.

Row 13 (RS) K5, *p5, k5; rep from * to end.

Row 14 P5, *k5, p5; rep from * to end. Rep rows 13 and 14 until piece measures 27"/68.5cm from beg, end with row 14.

KEYHOLE

Next row (RS) Work in rib pat over first 15 sts, join a 2nd ball of yarn, work in rib pat over last 50 sts. Working both sides at once, work even for 13 more rows.

Next (joining) row (RS) Work in rib pat over first 15 sts, with same ball of yarn, work in rib pat to end; cut 2nd ball of yarn. Cont to rep rows 13 and 14 until piece measures 29"/73.5cm from beg, end with row 14.

Next (inc) row (RS) K2, M1, k3, *p5, k2, M1, k3; rep from * to end—72 sts.

Row 15 (WS) P6, *k5, p6; rep from * to end.

Row 16 K6, *p5, k6; rep from * to end. Rep rows 15 and 16 until piece measures 32½"/82.5cm from beg, end with row 16.

Next (inc) row (WS) P6, *k2, M1, k3, p6; rep from * to end—78 sts.

Row 17 (RS) K6, *p6, k6; rep from * to end.

Row 18 P6, *k6, p6; rep from * to end. Rep rows 17 and 18 until piece measures 38"/96.5cm from beg, end with a WS row. Bind off loosely in rib pat. Do not block. ■

Basketweave Scarf

Knit in a deep charcoal gray, this simple scarf makes a strong statement. The easy basketweave pattern is so addictive, you won't want to make just one.

DESIGNED BY LINDA MEDINA

Finished measurements
Approx 6½" x 60"/16.5cm x 152.5cm

Materials
■ 2 3½oz/100g hanks (each approx 220yd/201m) of Cascade Yarns *220 Wool Heathers* (Peruvian highland wool) in #8400 charcoal grey
■ One pair size 7 (4.5mm) needles *or size to obtain gauge*

Note
Work each basketweave pat section very loosely. If it is pulling in too much, use a larger needle for that section only.

Scarf
Cast on 36 sts. Cont in pat sts as foll:
Rows 1 and 3 (RS) *K2, p1; rep from * to end.
Rows 2 and 4 *K1, p2; rep from * to end.
Rows 5–12 Knit.
Row 13 K4, *bring RH needle behind first st on LH needle and k 2nd st tbl (leave st on needle), then k first st, sl both sts from needle; rep from * to last 4 sts, end k4.
Row 14 K4, p1, *p 2nd st on LH needle (leave st on needle), then p first st, sl both sts from needle; rep from * to last 5 sts, end p1, k4.
Rows 15–20 Rep rows 13 and 14.
Rep rows 5–20 24 times more, end with a WS row. Rep rows 1–4 once more. Bind off in rib pat.

Finishing
Block piece to measurements. ■

Gauge
22 sts and 27 rows to 4"/10cm over basketweave pat using size 7 (4.5mm) needles.
Take time to check gauge.

Scalloped-Edge Beanie

This colorful cap fits tightly around the wearer's head, naturally curving at the cast-on edge. The delicate lace pattern and rosy hue add feminine flair.

DESIGNED BY CAROL SULCOSKI

EASY

Sizes
Instructions are written for one size.

Finished measurements
Circumference 20"/51cm
Depth 7"/17.5cm

Materials
■ 1 3½oz/100g hank (each approx 220yd/201m) of Cascade Yarns *220 Paints* (Peruvian highland wool) in #9842 coral beach

■ Size 8 (5mm) circular needle, 16"/40cm length *or size to obtain gauge*

■ One set (5) size 8 (5mm) double-pointed needles (dpns)

■ Stitch marker

Lace pattern
(multiple of 8 sts)
Rnd 1 Knit.

Rnd 2 *K1, yo, k2, SK2P, k2, yo, rep from * to end.
Rep rnds 1 and 2 for lace pat.

Hat
With circular needle, cast on 88 sts. Join and pm, taking care not to twist sts on needle. Cont in lace pat, rep rnds 1 and 2 nine times. Cont in St st until piece measures 6"/15cm from beg.

CROWN SHAPING
Change to dpns (dividing sts evenly between 4 needles) when there are too few sts on circular needle.
Dec rnd 1 *K6, k2tog, rep from * to end—77 sts.
Dec rnd 2 *K5, k2tog, rep from * to end—66 sts.
Dec rnd 3 *K4, k2tog, rep from * to end—55 sts.
Dec rnd 4 *K3, k2tog, rep from * to end—44 sts.
Dec rnd 5 *K2, k2tog, rep from * to end—33 sts.
Dec rnd 6 *K1, k2tog, rep from * to end—22 sts.
Dec rnd 7 *K2tog, rep from * to end—11 sts. Cut yarn, leaving an 8"/20.5cm tail and thread through rem sts. Pull tog tightly and secure end. ■

Gauge
20 sts and 24 rnds to 4"/10cm over St st using size 8 (5mm) needle.
Take time to check gauge.

Reverse Stockinette Mittens

These basic mittens are a perfect first project for aspiring mitten-knitters. The tweed cuff complements the solid hand and adds interest to the simple design.

DESIGNED BY LORI STEINBERG

Sizes
Instructions are written for one size.

Finished measurements
Hand circumference 7½"/19cm
Length of cuff approx 2½"/6.5cm

Materials
- 1 3½oz/100g hank (each approx 220yd/201m) of Cascade Yarns *220 Wool* (Peruvian highland wool) in #4002 jet (MC)
- 1 3½oz/100g hank (each approx 220yd/201m) of Cascade Yarns *220 Wool Quatro* (Peruvian highland wool) in #9540 charcoal twist (CC)
- One pair each size 5 (5.75mm) and 7 (4.5mm) needles *or size to obtain gauge*
- Stitch marker
- Tapestry needle

Note
Mittens are worked back and forth on straight needles and thumbs are worked in the rnd on dpns.

Stitch glossary
Inc 1 Knit into front and back of stitch.

Right mitten
CUFF
With smaller needles and CC, cast on 40 sts. Cont in rib pat as foll:
Row 1 (RS) *K1, p2; rep from *, end k1 (selvage st).
Row 2 K the knit sts and p the purl sts.
Rep last 2 rows until rib measures 2½"/6.5cm from beg, end with a RS row. Change to larger needles and MC.
Next row (WS) Inc 1 in first st, cont in rib pat to end—41 sts.

THUMB GUSSET
Set-up row (RS) P21, k1, p2, k1, p16.
Next row K the knit sts and p the purl sts.
Next (inc) row (RS) P to first k st, k1, M1 p-st, p2 to next k st, M1 p-st, k1, p to end—43 sts. Keeping st on either side of thumb gusset in St st and rem sts in reverse St st, rep inc row every 4th row 3 times more—49 sts. Work even until piece measures 5¼"/13.5cm from beg, end with a WS row.

HAND
Next row (RS) P to first k st, place next 12 sts on scrap yarn for thumb, cast on 4 sts, p to end—41 sts. Cont to work even in reverse St st until piece measures 8¾"/22cm from beg, end with a WS row.

TOP SHAPING
Dec row 1 (RS) P1, p2tog, p15, p2tog tbl, pm, p1, p2tog, p to last 3 sts, p2tog tbl, p1—37 sts. Knit next row.
Dec row 2 (RS) P1, p2tog, p to 2 sts before marker, p2tog tbl, slip marker, p1, p2tog, p to last 3 sts, p2tog tbl, p1—33 sts. Knit next row. Rep dec row 2 once more—29 sts.
Dec row 3 (WS) K1, SKP, k to 3 sts before marker, k2tog, k1, slip marker, k1, SKP, k to 3 sts before end, k2tog, k1—25 sts. Rep dec rows 2 and 3 once more—17 sts. Change to smaller needles.
Dec row 4 (RS) P1, [p2tog] 8 times—9 sts. Cut yarn leaving an 8"/20.5cm tail. Thread tail in tapestry needle, then thread through rem sts. Pull tog tightly and secure end.

THUMB
Place sts from scrap yarn on larger needle ready for RS row.
Next row (RS) P12, cast on 2 sts—14 sts.
Next row K14, cast on 2 sts—16 sts. Cont in rev St st until thumb measures 2"/5cm, end with RS row. Change to smaller needles.
(Continued on page 160.)

Gauge
21 sts and 29 rows to 4"/10cm over St st using larger needles. *Take time to check gauge.*

Cupcake Hat

Tempt your little girl's sweet tooth with this child-sized confection. You can change up the "frosting" color to match her favorite flavor.

DESIGNED BY LINDA MEDINA

■■■□ INTERMEDIATE

Sizes

Instructions are written for Child size Small.

Finished measurements

Circumference 16"/40.5cm
Depth 7¼"/18.5cm (excluding cherry)

Materials

■ 1 3½oz/100g ball (each approx 220yd/201m) of Cascade Yarns *220 Superwash* (superwash wool) each in #838 rose (MC), #872 bitter chocolate (A) and #809 really red (B)

■ One set (5) size 7 (4.5mm) double-pointed needles (dpns)

■ Stitch marker

Stitch glossary

kfb Knit in front and back of st—1 st increased.
Make bobble (MB) K1, p1, k1 in same st, making 3 sts from one; turn. P3, turn. K3, turn. P3, turn. K3, turn. Sl 1, p2tog, psso, turn. Sl st to RH needle.

Hat

With A, cast on 78 sts, dividing sts evenly over 4 needles. Join and pm, taking care not to twist sts on needles. Work in k2, p1 rib for 10 rnds. Change to MC.
Rnd (inc) 1 *Kfb in next st, k12; rep from * around—84 sts.
Rnd (inc) 2 *Kfb in next st, k20; rep from * around—88 sts.
Rnd 3 *K3, MB; rep from * around.
Rnd 4 Knit.
Rnd (inc) 5 *Kfb in next st, k10, pm; rep from * around—96 sts.
Rnds 6–8 Knit.
Rnd (inc) 9 *Kfb in next st, k11; rep from * around—104 sts.
Rnds 10–12 Knit.
Rnd (inc) 13 *Kfb in next st, k12; rep from * around—112 sts. Cont in St st until piece measures 4"/10cm from beg.

CROWN SHAPING

Dec rnd 1 *K2tog, k12; rep from * around—104 sts. Knit next rnd.
Dec rnd 2 *K2tog, k11; rep from * around—96 sts. Knit next rnd.
Dec rnd 3 *K2tog, k10; rep from * around—88 sts. Knit next rnd.
Dec rnd 4 *K2tog, k9; rep from * around—80 sts. Knit next rnd.
Dec rnd 5 *K2tog, k8; rep from * around—72 sts. Knit next rnd.
Dec rnd 6 *K2tog, k7; rep from * around—64 sts. Knit next rnd.
Dec rnd 7 *K2tog, k6; rep from * around—56 sts. Knit next rnd.
Dec rnd 8 *K2tog, k5; rep from * around—48 sts. Knit next rnd.
Dec rnd 9 *K2tog, k4; rep from * around—40 sts. Knit next rnd.
Dec rnd 10 *K2tog, k3; rep from * around—32 sts. Knit next rnd.
Dec rnd 11 *K2tog, k2; rep from * around—24 sts. Knit next rnd.
Dec rnd 12 *K2tog, k1; rep from * around—16 sts. Knit next rnd.
Dec rnd 13 [K2tog] 8 times—8 sts.
Cut yarn, leaving an 8"/20.5cm tail and thread through rem sts. Pull tog tightly and secure end.

Finishing

Referring to photo, embroider French knot "sprinkles" over top third of hat using A and B.

CHERRY

Roll a ball of B ⅞"/2cm in diameter. With B, cast on 10 sts. Work back and forth in St st for 1½"/4cm. Cut yarn, leaving an 18"/45.5cm tail and thread through sts. Pull tog, secure end, then sew side seam. Stuff yarn ball inside. Run needle through cast-on sts around bottom edge, pull tog tightly and secure end. Insert needle through center of ball. Make a small stitch, then insert needle down through center. Secure end. Sew cherry to top of hat. ■

FRENCH KNOT

Gauge

20 sts and 28 rnds to 4"/10cm over St st using size 7 (4.5mm) dpns. *Take time to check gauge.*

Eyelet Scarf

Look refined and proper in this genteel scarf knit in a serene hue. Perfect for a beginning lace project, it will boost your confidence in lace knitting in no time.

DESIGNED BY LISA BUCCELLATO

EASY

Finished measurements
Approx 5" x 40"/12.5cm x 101.5cm

Materials
■ 1 3½oz/100g hank (each approx 220yd/201m) of Cascade Yarns *220 Wool Quatro* (Peruvian highland wool) in #5016 shannon's pink

■ One pair size 7 (4.5mm) needles *or size to obtain gauge*

Lace pattern
(multiple of 6 sts plus 2)
Row 1 (RS) K2, *p1, yo, SKP, p1, k2; rep from * to end.
Row 2 *P2, k1; rep from *, end p2.
Row 3 K2, *p1, k2tog, yo, p1, k2; rep from * to end.
Row 4 Rep row 2.
Rep rows 1–4 for lace pat.

Scarf
Cast on 38 sts. Work even in lace pat until approx 36"/91.5cm of yarn rem, end with a RS row. Bind off in lace pat.

Finishing
Block piece lightly to measurements. ■

Gauge
30 sts and 29 rows to 4"/10cm over lace pat using size 7 (4.5mm) needles.
Take time to check gauge.

Garter-Ridged Hat

Knit in a beautiful variegated yarn, this cozy cap features contrasting garter-ridge stripes that really pop. It's perfect for a quick and easy gift!

DESIGNED BY KAREN GARLINGHOUSE

Sizes

Instructions are written for size Small/Medium. Changes for Large are in parentheses.

Finished measurements

Circumference 19½ (21½)"/ 49.5 (54.5)cm
Depth 7½ (7¾)"/19 (19.5)cm

Materials

■ 1 3½oz/100g hank (each approx 220yd/201m) of Cascade Yarns *220 Paints* (Peruvian highland wool) in #9849 harbour beach (MC)

■ 1 3½oz/100g hank (each approx 220yd/201m) of Cascade Yarns *220 Wool Heathers* (Peruvian highland wool) in #9459 yakima heather (CC)

■ Size 7 (4.5mm) circular needle, 16"/40cm length *or size to obtain gauge*

■ One set (4) size 7 (4.5mm) double-pointed needles (dpns)

■ Stitch marker

Hat

With circular needle and CC, cast on 88 (96) sts. Join and pm, taking care not to twist sts on needle. Knit next 4 rnds. Change to MC. Knit next 4 rnds. Change to CC. Cont in stripe pat as foll:
Rnd 1 Knit.
Rnd 2 Purl.
Rnd 3 Knit. Change to MC.
Rnds 4 and 5 Knit. Change to CC.
Rnds 6–8 Rep rnds 1–3. Change to MC.
Rnds 9 and 10 Knit.
Rnds 11–13 Rep rnds 1–3. Change to MC. Cont in St st until piece measures 5½ (6)"/14 (15)cm from beg.

CROWN SHAPING

Change to dpns (dividing sts evenly between 3 needles) when there are too few sts on circular needle.
Dec rnd 1 *K 9 (10), k2tog; rep from * around—80 (88) sts. Knit next rnd.
Dec rnd 2 *K 8 (9), k2tog; rep from * around—72 (80) sts. Knit next rnd.
Dec rnd 3 *K 7 (8), k2tog; rep from * around—64 (72) sts. Knit next rnd.
Dec rnd 4 *K 6 (7), k2tog; rep from * around—56 (64) sts. Knit next rnd.

Dec rnd 5 *K 5 (6), k2tog; rep from * around—48 (56) sts. Knit next rnd.
Dec rnd 6 *K 4 (5), k2tog; rep from * around—40 (48) sts. Knit next rnd.
Dec rnd 7 *K 3 (4), k2tog; rep from * around—32 (40) sts. Knit next rnd.
Dec rnd 8 *K 2 (3), k2tog; rep from * around—24 (32) sts. Knit next rnd.
Dec rnd 9 *K 1 (2), k2tog; rep from * around—16 (24) sts. Knit next rnd.

FOR LARGE SIZE ONLY

Dec rnd 10 *K1, k2tog; rep from * around—16 sts. Knit next rnd.

FOR BOTH SIZES

Next rnd *K2tog; rep from * around—8 sts. Cut yarn, leaving an 8"/20.5cm tail and thread through rem sts. Pull tog tightly and secure end. ■

Gauge

18 sts and 28 rnds to 4"/10cm over stripe pat using size 7 (4.5mm) circular needle.
Take time to check gauge.

Garter-Stitch Neck Wrap

A vintage-inspired neck wrap is the perfect canvas to showcase a favorite button. Knit in a solid with dashes of variegated yarn, this simple wrap gives you maximum impact with minimal effort.

DESIGNED BY JULIE GADDY

■■□□
EASY

Finished measurements
Approx 5½" x 35½"/14cm x 90cm (excluding fringe)

Materials
■ 1 3½oz/100g hank (each approx 220yd/201m) of Cascade Yarns *220 Wool* (Peruvian highland wool) in #9430 highland green (MC)

■ 1 3½oz/100g hank (each approx 220yd/201m) of Cascade Yarns *220 Wool Quatro* (Peruvian highland wool) in #9440 kauai (CC)

■ Size 8 (5mm) circular needle, 24"/61cm length *or size to obtain gauge*

■ One 1" x 1¾"/25mm x 44mm button

Notes
1) Scarf is knit horizontally from one long edge to opposite long edge.
2) Circular needle is used to accommodate the large number of sts. Do not join, but work back and forth in rows.
3) Fringe is made as you go by leaving a tail at beg and end of each row.

Scarf
With MC, loosely cast on 150 sts. Cut yarn, leaving a 4"/10cm tail; turn work. Cont in garter st and stripe pat as foll:

Rows 1–8 With MC, leave a 4"/10cm tail at beg of row and k to end. Cut yarn, leaving a 4"/10cm tail; turn work. AT THE SAME TIME, tie pairs of fringe tog as you go using an overhand knot. **Note** Do not trim fringe until scarf is completed.
Row 9 With CC, leave a 4"/10cm tail at beg row and k to end. Cut yarn, leaving a 4"/10cm tail; turn work.
Rows 10–14 Rep row 1.
Row 15 Rep row 9.
Rows 16–23 Rep row 1.
Row 24 Rep row 9.
Rows 25–27 Rep row 1.
Row (buttonhole) 28 (WS) With MC, leave a 4"/10cm tail at beg of row and k30, bind off next 5 sts, k to end. Cut yarn, leaving a 4"/10cm tail; turn work.
Row 29 Rep row 1, casting on 5 sts over bound-off sts.
Rows 30 and 31 Rep row 1.
Row 32 Rep row 9.
Rows 33–38 Rep row 1.
Row 39 Rep row 9.
Rows 40–47 Rep row 1.
Row 48 Rep row 9.
Rows 49–55 Rep row 1. Bind off all sts loosely knitwise. Cut yarn, leaving a 4"/10cm tail.

Finishing
Block piece lightly to measurements. Trim fringe to 1½"/4cm. At end opposite buttonhole, sew on button 7½"/19cm from side edge and centered top to bottom. ■

Gauge
17 sts and 42 rows to 4"/10cm over garter st using size 8 (5mm) needle.
Take time to check gauge.

Pocket Cap

Every child will love this hat, with a pouch perfectly sized for small treasures and treats. Knit the pocket lining in a contrasting color and bedeck with a favorite button or toggle.

DESIGNED BY KARI CAPONE

■■□□
EASY

Sizes
Instructions are written for Child size Small/Medium. Changes for Large are in parentheses.

Finished measurements
Circumference 16 (17¾)"/40.5 (45)cm
Depth 7¼ (7¾)"/18.5 (19.5)cm

Materials
■ 1 3½oz/100g hank (each approx 220yd/201m) of Cascade Yarns *220 Wool* (Peruvian highland wool) each in #9484 stratosphere (MC) and #7824 burnt orange (CC)

■ Size 7 (4.5mm) circular needle, 16"/40cm length *or size to obtain gauge*

■ One set (4) size 7 (4.5mm) double-pointed needles (dpns)

■ Stitch marker

■ Tapestry needle

Pocket lining
With dpns and CC, cast on 15 (17) st. Working back and forth on 2 needles, work in St st for 15 (17) rows. Set aside.

Hat
With circular needle and MC, cast on 72 (80) sts. Join and pm, taking care not to twist sts on needle. Work in k1, p1 rib for 8 rnds. Cont in St st and work even for 16 (18) rnds.

POCKET OPENING
Next rnd K 8 (12), bind off next 15 (17) sts, k to end.
Next rnd K 8 (12), hold pocket lining needle behind hat sts, with MC, p 15 (17) sts from pocket lining needle, k to end of rnd. Cont in St st for 8 rnds.

CROWN SHAPING
Change to dpns (dividing sts evenly between 3 needles) when there are too few sts on circular needle.
Rnd 1 *K 7 (8), k2tog; rep from * around—64 (72) sts. Knit next rnd.
Rnd 2 *K 6 (7), k2tog; rep from * around—56 (64) sts. Knit next rnd.
Rnd 3 *K 5 (6), k2tog; rep from * around—48 (56) sts. Knit next rnd.
Rnd 4 *K 4 (5), k2tog; rep from * around—40 (48) sts. Knit next rnd.
Rnd 5 *K 3 (4), k2tog; rep from * around—32 (40) sts. Knit next rnd.
Rnd 6 *K 2 (3), k2tog; rep from * around—24 (32) sts. Knit next rnd.
Rnd 7 *K 1 (2), k2tog; rep from * around—16 (24) sts. Knit next rnd.

FOR LARGE SIZE ONLY
Rnd 8 *K1, k2tog; rep from * around—16 sts.

FOR BOTH SIZES
Next rnd [K2tog] 8 times—8 sts.
Cut yarn leaving an 8"/20.5cm tail and thread through rem sts. Pull tog tightly and secure end.

POCKET FLAP
Turn hat so bottom edge is at top. With RS facing, dpns and MC, pick up and k 1 st in each of 15 (17) p sts along top of pocket lining. Working back and forth on 2 needles, cont as foll:
Rows 1 and 3 (WS) K1, p13 (15), k1.
Rows 2 and 4 Knit.
Row 5 Rep row 1.
Row (buttonhole) 6 (RS) K 6 (7), k2tog, yo, k7 (8).
Rows 7 and 8 Rep rows 1 and 2. Bind off all sts knitwise.

Finishing
Using MC, sew pocket lining in place. (Continued on page 160.)

Gauge
18 sts and 28 rnds to 4"/10cm over St st using size 7 (4.5mm) circular needle. *Take time to check gauge.*

Checkered Mittens

Inspired by classic houndstooth prints, these slip-stitch mittens have timeless appeal. Two shades of blue yarn combine for a subtle color pattern that spans fashion trends and seasons.

DESIGNED BY SUVI SIMOLA

Sizes
Instructions are written for one size.

Finished measurements
Hand circumference 7"/17.5cm
Length of cuff approx 2¾"/7cm

Materials
■ 1 3½oz/100g hank (each approx 220yd/201m) of Cascade Yarns *220 Wool* (Peruvian highland wool) each in #9332 sapphire (A) and #7815 summer sky (B)

■ One set (5) sizes 6 and 7 (4 and 4.5mm) double-pointed needles (dpns) *or size to obtain gauge*

■ Stitch markers

■ Tapestry needle

Stitch glossary
Jogless jog (worked on the next round after color change) When about to work the first st of a rnd, pick up loop of previous color under the first st, place it on LH needle, then knit the loop tog with the first st. The jogless jog creates a neat two-colored line of slipped sts along the side of palm and thumb.
M1R (make 1 right) Insert LH needle from *back* to *front* into the strand between last st worked and the next st on the LH needle. Knit into the front loop to twist the st.
M1L (make 1 left) Insert LH needle from *front to back* into the strand between last st worked and the next st on the LH needle. Knit into the back loop to twist the st.

Slip-stitch pattern
(multiple of 2 sts)
Rnd 1 With B, knit.
Rnd 2 With B, purl.
Rnd 3 With A, *sl 1 purlwise wyib, k1; rep from * around.
Rnd 4 With A, *sl 1 purlwise wyib, p1; rep from * around.
Rep rnds 1–4 for slip st pat.

Right mitten
CUFF
With smaller dpns and A, cast on 42 sts. Divide sts over 4 needles. Join taking care not to twist sts on needles, pm for beg of rnds. Cont in twisted rib pat as foll:
Next rnd *K1 tbl, p1; rep from * around. Rep this rnd until piece measures 2¾"/7cm from beg. Change to larger dpns and B. Set-up for thumb gusset as foll:
Rnd 1 With B, knit.

Rnd 2 With B, work first st as jogless jog, purl to end.
Rnd 3 With A, [k1, pm] twice, *sl 1 purlwise wyib, k1; rep from * around.
Rnd 4 With A, work first st as jogless jog, slip marker, p1, slip marker, *sl 1 purlwise wyib, p1; rep from * around.

THUMB GUSSET
Rnd (inc) 1 With B, k1, slip marker, M1R, k to next marker, M1L, slip marker, knit to end—44 sts.
Rnd 2 With B, work first st as jogless jog, purl to end.
Rnd 3 With A, k1, slip marker, k to next marker, slip marker, *sl 1 purlwise wyib, k1; rep from * around.
Rnd 4 With A, work first st as jogless jog, slip marker, purl to next marker, slip marker, *sl 1 purlwise wyib, p1; rep from around. Rep last 4 rnds 5 more times—54 sts (13 sts between markers).
Next rnd With B, k1, drop marker, place next 13 sts on scrap yarn for thumb, drop marker, cast on 3 sts, knit to end—44 sts.
Next rnd With B, work first st as jogless jog, purl to end.
Next (dec) rnd With A, k1, ssk, k1, *sl 1 purlwise wyib, k1; rep from * around—43 sts.
Next (dec) rnd With A, work first st as jogless jog, p2tog, *sl 1 purlwise wyib, p1; rep from * around—42 sts.

Gauge
20 sts and 48 rnds to 4"/10 cm over slip st pat using larger dpns. *Take time to check gauge.*

Checkered Mittens

HAND
Cont working slip st pat as foll:
Rnd 1 With B, knit.
Rnd 2 With B, work first st as jogless jog, purl to end.
Rnd 3 With A, k2, *sl 1 purlwise wyib, k1; rep from * around.
Rnd 4 With A, work first st as jogless jog, p1, *sl 1 purlwise wyib, p1; rep from * around. Rep rnds 1–4 until piece measures 5½"/14cm from last rnd of cuff, end with rnd 4.

TOP SHAPING
Rnd (dec) 1 With B, k2, ssk, k15, k2tog, k1, ssk, k15, k2tog, k1—38 sts.
Rnd (dec) 2 With B, work first st as jogless jog, p1, p2tog, p13, p2tog, p1, p2tog, p13, p2tog, p1—34 sts.
Rnd 3 With A, k2, *sl 1 purlwise wyib, k1; rep from * around.
Rnd 4 With A, work first st as jogless jog, p1, *sl 1 purlwise wyib, p1; rep from * around.
Rnd (dec) 5 With B, k2, ssk, k11, k2tog, k1, ssk, k11, k2tog, k1—30 sts.
Rnd (dec) 6 With B, work first st as jogless jog, p1, p2tog, p9, p2tog, p1, p2tog, p9, p2tog, p1—26 sts.
Rnd 7 With A, k2, *sl 1 purlwise wyib, k1; rep from * around.
Rnd 8 With A, work first st as jogless jog, p1, *sl 1 purlwise wyib, p1; rep from * around.
Rnd (dec) 9 With B, K2, ssk, k7, k2tog, k1, ssk, k7, k2tog, k1—22 sts.
Rnd (dec) 10 With B, work first st as jogless jog, p1, p2tog, p5, p2tog, p1, p2tog, p5, p2tog, p1—18 sts. Using B, graft sts tog using Kitchener st or 3-needle bind-off.

THUMB
Place 13 sts on scrap yarn over 3 needles.
Rejoin B, leaving a long tail for sewing.
Next rnd K13, pick up and k 3 sts over 3 cast-on sts—16 sts. Join and pm for beg of rnds.
Next rnd With B, work first st as jogless jog, purl to end. Cont working in garter st stripes as foll:
Rnd 1 With A, knit.
Rnd 2 With A, work first st as jogless jog, purl to end.
Rnd 3 With B, knit.
Rnd 4 With B, work first st as jogless jog, purl to end. Rep rnds 1–4 until thumb measures 1¾"/4.5cm.

TOP SHAPING
Rnd (dec) 1 With A, [k2, k2tog] 4 times—12 sts.
Rnd 2 With A, work first st as jogless jog, purl to end.
Rnd (dec) 3 With B, [k1, k2tog] 4 times—8 sts.
Rnd 4 With B, work first st as jogless jog, purl to end. Cut B, leaving a 6"/15cm tail. Thread tail in tapestry needle, then thread through rem sts. Pull tog tightly and secure end. Cut and weave in A on WS. Use yarn tail at base of thumb to close up any gaps between thumb and hand.

Left mitten
CUFF
Work as for right mitten. Change to larger dpns and B. Set-up for thumb gusset as foll:
Rnd 1 With B, knit.
Rnd 2 With B, work first st as jogless jog, purl to end.
Rnd 3 With A, k1, *k1, sl 1 purlwise wyib; rep from * to last st, end pm, k1.
Note The rnd marker will double as the 2nd of the 2 st markers used for the thumb gusset.

With A, work first st as jogless jog, *p1, sl 1 purlwise wyib; rep from * to last st, slip marker, p1.

THUMB GUSSET
Rnd (inc) 1 With B, knit to first marker, slip marker, M1R, knit to end, M1L—44 sts.
Rnd 2 With B, work first st as jogless jog, purl to end.
Rnd 3 With A, k1, *k1, sl 1 purlwise wyib; rep from * to marker, slip marker, k to end.
Rnd 4 With A, work first st as jogless jog, *p1, sl 1 purlwise wyib; rep from * to marker, slip marker, purl to end. Rep last 4 rnds 5 more times—54 sts (13 sts between markers).
Next rnd With B, knit to marker, drop marker, place next 13 sts on scrap yarn for thumb, cast on 3 sts—44 sts.
Next rnd With B, work first st as jogless joig, purl to end.
Next (dec) rnd With A, k1, *k1, sl 1 purlwise wyib; rep from * to last 3 sts, end k1, k2tog—43 sts.
Next (dec) rnd With A, work first st as jogless jog, *p1, sl 1 purlwise wyib; rep from * to last 2 sts, end p2tog—42 sts.

HAND
Work as for right mitten.

THUMB
Place 13 sts on scrap yarn over 3 needles. Rejoin B at beg of 3 sts cast-on above thumb opening, leaving a long tail for sewing.
Next rnd Pick up and k 3 sts over 3 cast-on sts, k13—16 sts. Join and pm for beg of rnds.
Next rnd With B, work first st as jogless jog, purl to end. Cont to work as for right mitten. ∎

Textured Tam

This softly shaped beret combines cabling and double moss stitch for a texture extravaganza.
Watch it all come to a point while knitting from the bottom up.

DESIGNED BY JACQUELINE VAN DILLEN

EXPERIENCED

Sizes
Instructions are written for one size.

Finished measurements
Circumference 20"/51cm
(slightly stretched)
Depth 8"/20.5cm

Materials
■ 1 3½oz/100g hank (each approx 220yd/201m) of Cascade Yarns *220 Wool* (Peruvian highland wool) in #8412 pear

■ Size 7 (4.5mm) circular needles, 16"/40cm length *or size to obtain gauge*

■ One set (5) size 7 (4.5mm) double-pointed needles (dpns)

■ Cable needle (cn)

■ Stitch marker

Note
To work in the rnd, always read chart from right to left.

Stitch glossary
2-st RC Sl 1 st to cn and hold to *back*, k1, k1 from cn.
4-st RC Sl 2 sts to cn and hold to *back*, k2, k2 from cn.
4-st RC with dec Sl 2 sts to cn and hold to *back*, k1, k2tog, then k2 from cn.

Hat
With smaller circular needle, cast on 94 sts. Join and pm, taking care not to twist sts on needle. Work in k1, p1 rib for 1¼"/3cm, inc 1 st at end of last rnd— 95 sts.

Gauge
21 sts and 28 rnds to 4"/10cm over St st using size 7 (4.5mm) circular needle.
Take time to check gauge.

Textured Tam

Beg chart pat
Beg on rnd 1 and work 19-st rep
5 times. Cont to work chart in this
manner through rnd 38, changing
to dpns (dividing sts evenly
between 4 needles) when there
are too few sts on circular
needle—10 sts.
Next rnd [K2tog] 5 times—5 sts.
Cut yarn, leaving a 6"/15cm tail
and thread through rem sts.
Pull tog tightly and secure end. ■

Stitch Key

☐   K on RS

—   P on RS

▨   No stitch

Ⓞ   Yo

⟋   K2tog

⟍   P2tog tbl

⟋   P2tog

↟   SK2P

⟋   2-st RC

⟍⟍   4-st RC

⟍⟍   4-st RC with dec

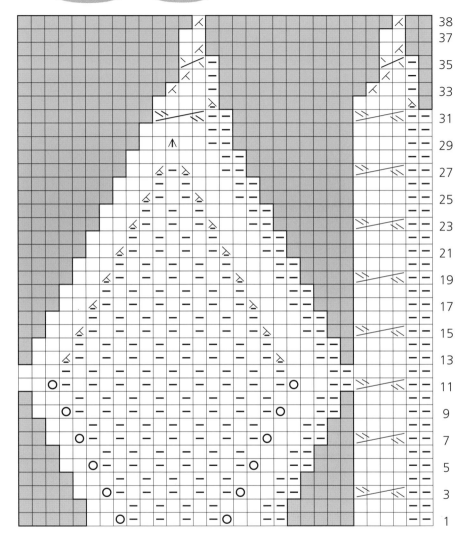

✳ Quick Tip
Add a pompom to the top of this tam in the same shade
as the main hat or in a contrasting color for a kick.

36

Leaf Scarf

Cultivate a refined wardrobe with this trellis-like leaf scarf. Featuring embossed leaves on a backdrop of garter stitch, it'll grow on you!

DESIGNED BY MARY BETH TEMPLE

■■□ INTERMEDIATE

Finished measurements

Approx 7" x 64"/17.5cm x 162.5cm

Materials

■ 2 3½oz/100g hanks (each approx 220yd/201m) of Cascade Yarns *220 Wool Heathers* (Peruvian highland wool) in #2422 lavender

■ One pair size 7 (4.5mm) needles *or size to obtain gauge*

Scarf

Cast on 33 sts. Cont in pat sts as foll:
Rows 1–6 Knit.
Rows 7 (RS) K5, [ssk, k2, yo, k1, yo, k2, k2tog, k5] twice.
Row 8 and all WS rows K5 [p9, k5] twice.
Rows 9 and 11 Rep row 7.
Row 13 K5, [yo, ssk, k5, k2tog, yo, k5] twice.
Row 15 K6, yo, ssk, k3, k2tog, yo, k7, yo, ssk, k3, k2tog, yo, k6.
Row 17 K7, yo, ssk, k1, k2tog, yo, k9, yo, ssk, k1, k2tog, yo, k7.
Row 19 K8, yo, SK2P, yo, k11, yo, SK2P, yo, k8.
Row 20 Rep row 8.
Rep rows 7–20 for leaf pat and work even until piece measures 63"/160cm from beg, end with row 7.
Knit next 6 rows. Bind off all sts loosely knitwise.

Finishing

Block piece lightly to measurements. ■

Gauge

19 sts and 28 rows to 4"/10cm over leaf pat using size 7 (4.5mm) needles.
Take time to check gauge.

Mock Cable Wristers

These blushing beauties will warm the hands and heart of any lucky recipient. With a wide, dramatic faux cable and ribbed openings, they're also definite eye-catchers.

DESIGNED BY ANNE FARNHAM

INTERMEDIATE

Sizes
Instructions are written for one size.

Finished measurements
Hand circumference 7"/17.5cm
Length of cuff approx 1¼"/3cm

Materials
■ 1 3½oz/100g hank (each approx 220yd/201m) of Cascade Yarns *220 Wool Heathers* (Peruvian highland wool) in #9442 baby rose heather

■ One set (4) size 6 (4mm) double-pointed needles (dpns) *or size to obtain gauge*

■ Stitch markers

Stitch glossary
pfbf Purl in front, back and front of st—2 sts increased.

Mock cable panel
(worked over 14 sts)
Rnd 1 Yo, k3, ssk, k9.
Rnd 2 K1, yo, k3, ssk, k8.
Rnd 3 K2, yo, k3, ssk, k7.
Rnd 4 K3, yo, k3, ssk, k6.
Rnd 5 K4, yo, k3, ssk, k5.
Rnd 6 K5, yo, k3, ssk, k4.
Rnd 7 K6, yo, k3, ssk, k3.
Rnd 8 K7, yo, k3, ssk, k2.
Rnd 9 K8, yo, k3, ssk, k1.
Rnd 10 K9, yo, k3, ssk.
Rep rnds 1–10 for mock cable panel.

Left wrister
CUFF
With dpns, cast on 38 sts and divide sts evenly over 3 needles. Join, taking care not to twist sts on needles, pm for beg of rnds. Work around in k1, p1 rib for 1¼"/3cm.

HAND
Cont in mock cable panel and reverse St st as foll:
Rnd 1 P12, pm, work mock cable panel over next 14 sts, pm, p to end.
Rnd 2 P12, sl marker, work mock cable panel over next 14 sts, sl marker, p to end. Keeping sts each side of markers in reverse St st and rem sts in mock cable panel, work even for 5 rnds more.

THUMB GUSSET
Inc rnd 1 P9, pm (for gusset), pfbf, pm (for gusset), work to end—40 sts. Work next rnd even.
Inc rnd 2 Work to first gusset marker, sl marker, M1 p-st, p to next gusset marker, M1 p-st, sl marker, work to end—42 sts. Work next rnd even. Rep last 2 rnds until there are 13 sts between gusset markers-50 sts.
Work next 3 rnds even.
Next rnd Work to first gusset marker, drop marker, bind off next 12 sts, drop marker, work to end—38 sts. Work even until piece measures 4¾"/12cm from beg, dropping mock cable panel markers on last rnd. Cont in k1, p1 rib for 6 rnds; piece should measure approx ¾"/14.5cm from beg. Bind off in rib pat.

Right wrister
Work as for left wrister to thumb gusset.

THUMB GUSSET
Inc rnd 1 Work across first 28 sts, pm (for gusset), pfbf, pm (for gusset), work to end—40 sts. Work next rnd even. Beg with inc rnd 2, cont to work as for left wrister. ■

Gauge
22 sts and 28 rnds to 4"/10cm over reverse St st using size 6 (4mm) dpns.
Take time to check gauge.

Garter-Ridged Scarf

Simple stockinette stripes alternate with garter-ridge stripes in this warm and cozy lengthwise-knit muffler. Vary the colors to customize it for everyone on your list!

DESIGNED BY LYNN WILSON

EASY

Finished measurements
Approx 5½" x 59¼"/14cm x 150.5cm

Materials
■ 1 3½oz/100g hank (each approx 220yd/201m) of Cascade Yarns *220 Wool Heathers* (Peruvian highland wool) each in #2448 mallard (A) and #9489 red wine heather (B)

■ Size 8 (5mm) circular needle, 24"/61cm length *or size to obtain gauge*

Notes
1) Scarf is knit horizontally from one long edge to opposite long edge.
2) Circular needle is used to accommodate the large number of sts. Do not join, but work back and forth in rows.
3) Carry yarns not in use loosely up RH side.

Scarf
With A, loosely cast on 260 sts.
Rows 1–6 Sl 1 knitwise wyib, k to end. Change to B.
Row 7 (RS) Purl.

Row 8 Purl.
Rows 9 and 11 Sl 1 knitwise wyib, k to end.
Rows 10 and 12 Sl 1 purlwise wyif, p to end. Change to A.
Row 13 Purl.
Row 14 Knit. Change to B. Rep rows 7–14 twice more, then rows 7–12 once. Change to A.
Row 37 Purl.
Rows 38–42 Sl 1 knitwise wyib, k to end. Bind off all sts loosely knitwise.

Finishing
Block piece lightly to measurements. ■

Quick Tip
This project is perfect for new knitters! Build up your confidence by adding a few new skills to your repertoire.

Gauge
22 sts to 5"/12.5cm and 30 rows to 4"/10cm over stripe pat using size 8 (5mm) needle.
Take time to check gauge.

Cables & Stripes Mittens

These green-and-blue delights are a touch of spring in the middle of winter. Cables set against reverse stockinette with color changes every eight rows make them as fun to knit as they are to wear.

DESIGNED BY JANE DUPUIS

◼◼◼▢
INTERMEDIATE

Sizes
Instructions are written for one size.

Finished measurements
Hand circumference 7½"/19cm
Length of cuff approx 1¼"/3cm

Materials
■ 1 3½oz/100g hank (each approx 220yd/201m) of Cascade Yarns *220 Wool* (Peruvian highland wool) each in #7812 lagoon (A), #2409 palm (B), #9420 como blue (C), #8903 primaverra (D), #9427 duck egg blue (E), #9076 mint (F), #8902 herb (G), #8910 citron (H) and #8908 anis (I)

■ Contrasting heavy worsted-weight yarn (waste yarn)

■ One set (5) size 6 (4mm) double-pointed needles (dpns) *or size to obtain gauge*

■ Cable needle (cn)

■ Stitch markers

Note
The back of hand is worked in a broken cable pat, and palm and thumb are worked in St st. All follow the same stripe sequence.

Stitch glossary
4-st LC Sl 2 sts to cn and hold to *front*, k2, k2 from cn.

Twisted rib pattern
(multiple of 3 sts)
Rnd 1 *K2 tbl, p1; rep from * around.
Rep rnd 1 for twisted rib pat.

Left mitten
CUFF
With dpns and A, cast on 42 sts. Divide sts over 4 needles as foll: 12 sts on needles 1 and 2 and 9 sts on needles 3 and 4. Join, taking care not to twist sts on needles, pm for beg of rnds. Work in twisted rib pat for 8 rnds. Rearrange sts on needles as foll: move 1 st from end of needle 1 to beg of needle 2 (11 sts rem on needle 1); move 2 sts from end of needle 2 to beg of needle 3 (11 sts rem on needle 2); move 1 st from end of needle 3 to beg of needle 4 (10 sts rem on both needles 3 and 4). Change to B.

HAND
Note Back of hand will be worked in broken cable pat over 22 sts across needles 1 and 2; palm of hand will be worked in St st over 20 sts across needles 3 and 4. Cont as foll:
Rnds 1–3 K1, p4, k4, p4, k4, p4, k21.
Rnd 4 K1, p4, 4-st LC, p4, 4-st LC, p4, k21.
Rnds 5–7 Rep rnd 1. Change to C.
Rnds 8–10 P1, k4, p4, k4, p4, k4, p1, k20.
Rnd 11 P1, 4-st LC, p4, 4-st LC, p4, 4-st LC, p1, k20.
Rnds 12–14 Rep rnd 8. Change to D and rep rnds 1–7. Change to E and rep rnd 8.

THUMB PLACEMENT
Next rnd P1, k4, p4, k4, p4, k4, p1, k12, k6 onto waste yarn, sl these 6 sts back to LH needle; cont with E, knit these 6 sts again, k2. Rep rnds 10–14. Change to F and rep rnds 1–7. Change to G and rep rnds 8–14. Change to H and rep rnds 1–5.

TOP SHAPING
Rnd (dec) 1 SKP, p3, k4, p4, k4, p3, k2tog, SKP, k16, k2tog—38 sts.

Gauge
20 sts and 28 rnds to 4"/10cm over St st using size 6 (4mm) dpns.
Take time to check gauge.

Cables & Stripes Mittens

Rnd (dec) 2 SKP, p2, k4, p4, k4, p2, k2tog, SKP, k14, k2tog—34 sts. Change to I.

Rnd (dec) 3 SKP, k1, p4, k4, p4, k1, k2tog, SKP, k12, k2tog—30 sts.

Rnd (dec) 4 SKP, p4, k4, p4, k2tog, SKP, k10, k2tog—26 sts.

Rnd (dec) 5 SKP, p3, k4, p3, k2tog, SKP, k8, k2tog—22 sts.

Rnd (dec) 6 SKP, p2, 4-st LC, p2, k2tog, SKP, k6, k2tog—18 sts.

Rnd (dec) 7 SKP, p1, k4, p1, k2tog, SKP, k4, k2tog—14 sts.

Rnd (dec) 8 SKP, k4, k2tog, SKP, k2, k2tog—10 sts.

Rnd (dec) 9 SKP, k2, k2tog, SKP, k2tog—6 sts. Cut yarn, leaving an 8"/20.5cm tail and thread through rem sts. Pull tog tightly and secure end.

THUMB

Place 6 sts below waste yarn on needle 1 and 6 sts above waste yarn on needle 3. Join E, k 6 sts on needle 1, with needle 2 pick up and k 2 sts along side edge of opening, k 6 sts on needle 3, with needle 4 pick up and k 2 sts along side edge of opening—16 sts. Divide sts evenly between 4 needles. Join and pm for beg od rnds. Knit 6 rnds. Change to F and knit 7 rnds. Change to H and knit 3 rnds. Cont with H as foll:

TOP SHAPING

Rnd 1 [K2tog, k4, k2tog] twice—12 sts.

Rnd 2 [K2tog, k2, k2tog] twice—8 sts.

Rnd 3 [K2tog] 4 times—4 sts.

Cut yarn, leaving an 8"/20.5cm tail and thread through rem sts. Pull tog tightly and secure end.

Right mitten

Work as for left mitten to thumb placement.

THUMB PLACEMENT

Next rnd P1, k4, p4, k4, p4, k4, p1, k2, k6 onto waste yarn, sl these 6 sts back to LH needle; cont with E, knit these 6 sts again, k12. Cont to work as for left mitten. ■

Quick Tip

If changing colors intimidates you, use just two colors. Carry the yarns on the inside without cutting, and you won't have to worry about weaving in many ends.

Tweed Mittens

Opposites attract in these textured mitts. By switching up the colors post-cuff, dark becomes light and creates an eye-catching illusion.

DESIGNED BY NICHOLE REESE

Sizes
Instructions are written for one size.

Finished measurements
Hand circumference 7½"/19cm
Length of cuff approx 2¾"/7cm

Materials
■ 1 3½oz/100g hank (each approx 220yd/201m) of Cascade Yarns *220 Wool* (Peruvian highland wool) each in #8010 natural (MC) and #8400 charcoal grey (CC)

■ Contrasting heavy worsted-weight yarn (waste yarn)

■ One set (4) size 7 (4.5mm) double-pointed needles (dpns) *or size to obtain gauge*

■ Stitch marker

■ Tapestry needle

Note
To work in the rnd, always read charts from right to left.

Right mitten
CUFF
With dpns and CC, cast on 42 sts. Divide sts over 3 needles (14 sts on each). Join, taking care not to twist sts on needles, pm for beg of rnds. Purl next rnd.
Beg chart pat I
Rnd 1 Work 3-st rep 14 times. Cont to work in this way to rnd 6, then rep rnds 1–6 four times more.

Gauge
24 sts and 34 rnds to 4"/10cm over chart pat using size 7 (4.5mm) dpns.
Take time to check gauge.

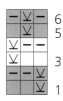

Chart I

−	∨	−	6
	∨		5
∨	−	−	3
∨			
−	−	∨	
		∨	1

Chart II

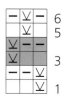

−	∨	−	6
	∨		5
∨	−	−	3
∨			
−		∨	
		∨	1

3 2 1

Color Key

☐ Natural (MC)

▨ Charcoal grey (CC)

Stitch Key

☐ K on RS

⊟ P on RS

▽ Sl 1 wyib

HAND

Next rnd With CC, M1, k to end—43 sts.
Next rnd With CC, p1, M1 p-st, p to end—44 sts.
Beg chart pat II
Rnd 1 With MC, sl 1 wyib, k1, M1, beg with st 1, work 3-st rep 14 times—45 sts.
Rnd 2 Work 3-st rep 15 times. Cont to work in this way to rnd 6, then rep rnds 1–6 four times more.

THUMB PLACEMENT

Next rnd With MC, sl 1 wyib, k1, k9 onto waste yarn, sl these 9 sts back to LH needle, with MC, k these 9 sts again, then k1; beg on rnd 1 and st 1, work 3-st rep 11 times.
Rnd 2 Work 3-st rep 15 times. Cont to work in this way to rnd 6, then rep rnds 1–6 seven times more.

TOP SHAPING

Rnd (dec) 1 With MC, *[sl 1 wyib, k2] 3 times, sl 1 wyib, k1, k4tog; rep from * around twice more—36 sts.
Rnd 2 With MC, [sl 1 wyib, p2] 12 times.
Rnd 3 With CC, [k2, sl 1 wyib] 12 times.
Rnd 4 With CC, [p2, sl 1 wyib] 12 times.
Rnd (dec) 5 With MC, *k4tog, sl 1 wyib, k1, [k1, sl 1 wyib, k1] twice; rep from * around twice more—27 sts.
Rnd 6 With MC, [p1, sl 1 wyib, p1] 9 times.
Rnd (dec) 7 With MC, [sl 1 wyib, k2, sl 1 wyib, k1, k4tog] 3 times—18 sts.
Rnd 8 With MC, [sl 1 wyib, p2] 6 times.
Rnd 9 With CC, [k2, sl 1 wyib] 6 times.
Rnd 10 With CC [p2, sl 1 wyib] 6 times.
Rnd (dec) 11 With MC, [k4tog, sl 1 wyib, k1] 3 times—9 sts.

Rnd 12 With MC, [p1, sl 1 wyib, k1] 3 times. Cut MC, leaving a 6"/15.5cm tail. Thread tail in tapestry needle, then thread through rem sts. Pull tog tightly and secure end. Cut and weave in CC on WS.

THUMB

Remove waste yarn and place 18 live sts on 2 dpns with 9 sts below thumb opening on one needle and 9 sts above opening on a 2nd needle, then divide sts over 3 needles (6 sts on each). Join and pm for beg of rnds. Join MC at RH side of bottom needle, leaving a long tail for sewing.
Beg chart pat II
Rnd 1 Work 3-st rep 6 times.
Cont to work in this way to rnd 6, then rep rnds 1–6 three times more, then work rnds 1–4 once.

TOP SHAPING

Rnd (dec) 1 With MC, [k4tog, sl 1 wyib, k1] 3 times—9 sts.
Rnd 2 With MC, [p1, sl 1 wyib, k1] 3 times. Cut MC, leaving a 6"/15.5cm tail. Thread tail in tapestry needle, then thread through rem sts. Pull tog tightly and secure end. Cut and weave in CC on WS. Use yarn tail at base of thumb to close up any gaps between thumb and hand.

Left mitten

Work as for right mitten to thumb placement.

THUMB PLACEMENT

Next rnd With MC, [sl 1 wyib, k2] 3 times, sl 1 wyib, k1, k9 onto waste yarn, sl these 9 sts back to LH needle, with MC, k these 9 sts again, then k1; *sl 1 wyib, k1; rep from * around. Cont to work as for right mitten. ▪

Pocket Scarf

Girls (or guys) on the go need to keep their hands free. Stash tissues, your music player or your good-luck charm in this simple double-knit, garter-edge scarf that is as functional as it is fun.

DESIGNED BY CATHY CARRON

EASY

Finished measurements

Approx 5¼" x 74"/13cm x 188cm

Materials

■ 1 3½oz/100g hank (each approx 220yd/201m) of Cascade Yarns *220 Wool Heathers* (Peruvian highland wool) each in #2452 turtle (A) and #9459 yakima heather (B)

■ One pair size 7 (4.5mm) needles *or size to obtain gauge*

■ Two 1"/25mm buttons

Scarf

POCKET LINING SECTION

With A, cast on 30 sts. Knit next 10 rows. Work in pat st as foll:

Row 1 (WS) [K6, p6] twice, k6.

Row 2 Knit. Rep last 2 rows 17 times.

Note The WS of the pocket lining now becomes the RS of the center section.

CENTER SECTION

Next row (RS) Knit.

Next row (WS) [K6, p6] twice, k6. Rep last 2 rows until piece measures 37"/94cm from beg, end with a WS row. Change to B.

Next row (RS) Knit.

Next row (WS) [K6, p6] twice, k6. Rep last 2 rows until piece measures 68"/172.5cm, end with a RS row.

Note The WS of the center section now becomes the RS of the pocket lining.

POCKET LINING SECTION

Next row (RS) Knit.

Next row (WS) [K6, p6] twice, k6. Rep last 2 rows 17 times more. Knit next 10 rows. Bind off all sts knitwise.

Pockets (make 2)

With A, cast on 30 sts. Knit next 10 rows. Work in pat st as foll:

Row 1 (WS) K7, p16, k7.

Row 2 (RS) Knit. Rep last 2 rows 17 times more, then row 1 once more.

Next (buttonhole) row (RS) K13, bind off next 4 sts, k to end.

Next row K7, p6, cast on 4 sts, p6, k7. Knit next 10 rows. Bind off all sts knitwise. Make another pocket using B.

Finishing

Block pieces lightly to measurements. Position WS of pocket A on WS of pocket lining section B (RS of scarf), so bottom and side edges are even. Cut a 50"/127cm length of B. Using B doubled in tapestry needle, sew pocket in place using running stitch along the inside edge of the garter st border as foll: beg at upper RH corner, stitch down to lower RH corner, across bottom, then up to upper LH corner. Now working through pocket fabric only, stitch across to upper RH corner, making sure to stitch above buttonhole. Secure ends on WS. Using A (same color as pocket), tack each corner of pocket to scarf. Working in the same manner, sew rem pocket to opposite end of scarf. Sew on buttons. ■

RUNNING STITCH

Gauge

23 sts and 29 rows to 4"/10cm over pat sts using size 7 (4.5mm) needle.
Take time to check gauge.

Ribbed Pillbox

Stretchy ribbing makes this hat a winner for all sizes. With a top that forms a square, this flattering head-hugger is a modern take on the classic pillbox.

DESIGNED BY CAROL SULCOSKI

EASY

Sizes
Instructions are written for one size.

Finished measurements
Circumference 19"/48.5cm
(slightly stretched)
Depth 8"/20.5cm

Materials
- 1 3½oz/100g hank (each approx 220yd/201m) of Cascade Yarns *220 Wool Heathers* (Peruvian highland wool) in #2429 irelande
- Size 7 (4.5mm) circular needle, 16"/40cm length *or size to obtain gauge*
- One set (5) size 7 (4.5mm) double-pointed needles (dpns)
- Stitch marker

Hat
With circular needle, cast on 100 sts. Join and pm, taking care not to twist sts on needle. Work around in k3, p2 rib until piece measures 5½"/14cm from beg.
Next (dec) rnd *K8, p2tog; rep from * around—90 sts. Purl next 4 rnds.
Next (dec) rnd *K7, k2tog; rep from * around—80 sts. Knit next 3 rnds.

CROWN SHAPING
Change to dpns (dividing sts evenly between 4 needles) when there are too few sts on circular needle.
Dec rnd 1 K8, [ssk, k2tog, k16] 3 times, ssk, k2tog, k8—72 sts.
Dec rnd 2 K7, [ssk, k2tog, k14] 3 times, ssk, k2tog, k7—64 sts.
Dec rnd 3 K6, [ssk, k2tog, k12] 3 times, ssk, k2tog, k6—56 sts.
Dec rnd 4 K5, [ssk, k2tog, k10] 3 times, ssk, k2tog, k5—48 sts.
Dec rnd 5 K4, [ssk, k2tog, k8] 3 times, ssk, k2tog, k4—40 sts.
Dec rnd 6 K3, [ssk, k2tog, k6] 3 times, ssk, k2tog, k3—32 sts.
Dec rnd 7 K2, [ssk, k2tog, k4] 3 times, ssk, k2tog, k2—24 sts.
Dec rnd 8 K1, [ssk, k2tog, k2] 3 times, ssk, k2tog, k1—16 sts. Drop marker.
Dec rnd 9 [Ssk, k2tog] 4 times—8 sts. Cut yarn, leaving an 8"/20.5cm tail and thread through rem sts. Pull tog tightly and secure end. ■

Gauge
20 sts and 30 rnds to 4"/10cm over rib pat using size 7 (4.5mm) needle (slightly stretched).
Take time to check gauge.

Octopus Mittens

Bring a little undersea enchantment to the surface with these child-sized mitts. Knit in Fair Isle in Technicolor shades of blue and green, they're sure to please waterbabies and landlubbers alike.

DESIGNED BY ELLI STUBENRAUCH

EXPERIENCED

Sizes
Instructions are written for Child size Small.

Finished measurements
Hand circumference 5½"/14cm
Length of cuff approx 2¼"/5.5cm

Materials
■ 1 3½oz/100g ball (each approx 220yd/201m) of Cascade Yarns *220 Superwash* (superwash wool) each in #886 citron (A) and #812 turquoise (B)
■ Contrasting heavy worsted-weight yarn (waste yarn)
■ One set (5) each size 5 and 6 (3.75 and 4mm) double-pointed needles (dpns) *or size to obtain gauge*
■ Stitch marker

Note
To work in the rnd, always read charts from right to left.

Stitch glossary
Kfb Knit in front and back of st—1 st increased.

M1R (make 1 right) Insert left needle from *back* to *front* into the horizontal strand between the last st worked and the next st on left needle. Using color indicated on chart, knit this strand through the front loop to twist the st.
M1L (make 1 left) Insert left needle from *front* to *back* into the horizontal strand between the last st worked and the next st on left needle. Using color indicated on chart, knit this strand through the back loop to twist the st.

Corrugated rib
(multiple of 2 sts)
Rnd 1 *P1 with B, k1 with A; rep from * around.
Rep rnd 1 for corrugated rib.

Left mitten
CUFF
With smaller dpns and A, cast on 28 sts. Divide sts over 4 needles (7 sts on each). Join, taking care not to twist sts on needles, pm for beg of rnds. Cont in corrugated rib for 14 rnds. Change to larger dpns.
Next (inc) rnd [K1 with B, k1 with A] twice, kfb with B, [k1 with A, k1 with B] twice, k1 with A, kfb with B, [k1 with A, k1 with B] twice, with A (k2, kfb, k5, kfb, k4)—32 sts. Cont in St st as foll:

Beg chart pat I
Beg chart on rnd 1 and work even through rnd 2.

THUMB GUSSET
Rnd 3 With B, M1R, k1, M1L, work to end of rnd—34 sts. Cont to foll chart in this way through rnd 13, working inc as shown—44 sts.
Rnd 14 Place 12 thumb sts on scrap yarn. Cont to work to top of chart, dec top of mitten as shown—20 sts. Cut A, leaving a 12"/30.5cm tail. Place 10 sts from front on one needle and 10 sts from back on a 2nd needle. Graft sts tog using Kitchener st or 3-needle bind-off.

THUMB
Place 12 sts on scrap yarn evenly over 4 needles (3 sts on each). Pm for beg of rnds. Rejoin B, leaving a long tail for sewing.
Beg chart II
Beg chart on rnd 1 and work to top of of chart, inc and dec as shown—12 sts.
Next rnd With B, [ssk] 6 times—6 sts. Cut B, leaving a 6"/15.5cm tail. Thread tail in tapestry needle, then thread through rem sts. Pull tog tightly and secure end.

Gauge
23 sts and 26 rnds to 4"/10cm over chart pat using larger dpns (after blocking). *Take time to check gauge.*

Octopus Mittens

Chart I

Color Key

☐ Citron (A)

☐ Turquoise (B)

Stitch Key

☐ No stitch

Ⓨ M1R

Ⓨ M1L

Ⓧ K2tog

Ⓧ Ssk

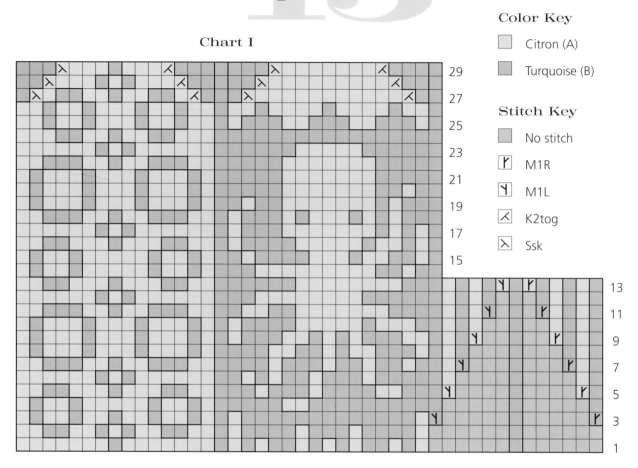

Chart II

Right mitten
CUFF
Work as for left mitten to inc rnd.

Next (inc) rnd K1 with B, with A (k2, kfb, k5, kfb, k4), [k1 with B, k1 with A] twice, kfb with B, [k1 with A, k1 with B] twice, k1 with A, kfb with B, k1 with A, k1 with B, k1 with A—32 sts. Cont to work as for left mitten, foll chart III for hand and chart II for thumb.

Finishing
For each mitten, use B tail to sew gap between thumb and hand closed. Block pieces to measurements. ■

Chart III

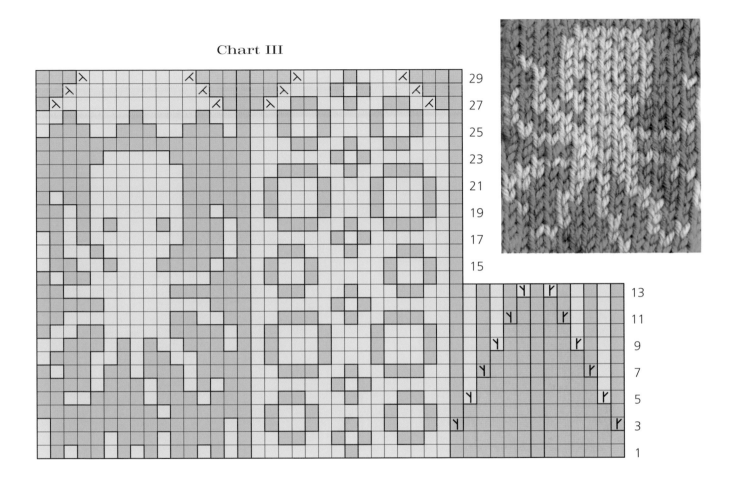

Tasseled Topper

Dual tassels, garter ridges and a cabled center panel keep things interesting. With multiple techniques, this hat is perfect for the knitter ready to advance beyond a beginner level.

DESIGNED BY LINDA MEDINA

◼◼◼◻
INTERMEDIATE

Sizes
Instructions are written for one size.

Finished measurements
Circumference 21"/53.5cm
(slightly stretched)
Depth 8"/20.5cm

Materials
- 1 3½oz/100g hank (each approx 220yd/201m) of Cascade Yarns *220 Wool* (Peruvian highland wool) in #8114 dusty rose
- Size 7 (4.5mm) circular needle, 16"/40cm length *or size to obtain gauge*
- One set (5) size 7 (4.5mm) double-pointed needles (dpns)
- Cable needle (cn)
- Stitch markers

Stitch glossary
8-st RPC Sl 4 sts to cn and hold to *back*, k1, p2, k1, then k1, p2, k1 from cn.
8-st LPC Sl 4 sts to cn and hold to *front*, k1, p2, k1, then k1, p2, k1 from cn.

Hat
With circular needle, cast on 108 sts. Join and pm, taking care not to twist sts on needle. Work in k2, p1 rib for 1½"/4cm. Cont in pat st as foll:
Rnd 1 P4, k1, [p2, k2] 3 times, p2, k1, p4, pm, k to end.
Rnds 2–5 Rep rnd 1.
Rnd 6 P4, k1, [p2, k2] 3 times, p2, k1, p4, slip marker, p to end.
Rnd 7 P4, 8-st RPC, 8-st LPC, p4, sl marker, p to end.
Rnds 8–11 Rep rnd 1.
Rnd 12 Rep rnd 6.
Rnds 13–16 Rep rnd 1.
Rnd 17 P4, 8-st RPC, 8-st LPC, p4, sl marker, k to end.
Rnd 18 Rep rnd 1.
Rnd 19 Rep rnd 6.
Rnds 20 and 21 Rep rnd 1.
Rnd 22 Purl, dropping 2nd second marker.
Rnd 23 Purl.
Rnds 24–26 Knit.
Rnd 27 Purl.
Rnds 28–32 Knit.
Rnds 33 and 34 Purl.

CROWN SHAPING
Change to dpns as foll:
Dec rnd 1 *With dpn, [k2tog] 13 times, k1; rep from * 3 times more-—56 sts (14 sts on each needle).
Dec rnd 2 *K12, k2tog; rep from * around—52 sts.
Dec rnd 3 *K11, k2tog; rep from * around—48 sts.
Dec rnd 4 *K10, k2tog; rep from * around—44 sts.
Dec rnd 5 *K9, k2tog; rep from * around—40 sts.
Dec rnd 6 *K8, k2tog; rep from * around—36 sts.
Dec rnd 7 *K7, k2tog; rep from * around—32 sts.
Dec rnd 8 *K6, k2tog; rep from * around—28 sts.
Dec rnd 9 *K5, k2tog; rep from * around—24 sts.
Dec rnd 10 *K4, k2tog; rep from * around—20 sts.
Dec rnd 11 *K3, k2tog; rep from * around—16 sts.
Dec rnd 12 *K2, k2tog; rep from * around—12 sts.
Dec rnd 13 *K1, k2tog; rep from * around—8 sts. Cut yarn, leaving an 8"/20.5cm tail and thread through rem sts. Pull tog tightly and secure end.

Tassels (make 2)
Wrap yarn 85 times around a 5"/12.5cm piece of cardboard. Slip two 12"/30.5cm-lengths of yarn under strands and tightly knot at one end of cardboard. Remove cardboard. Wrap another length of yarn 8 times around the tassel about 1"/2.5cm down from the top. Cut loops at opposite ends. Trim ends even. Sew tassels to top of hat, as shown. ◼

Gauge
21 sts and 24 rnds to 4"/10cm over pat st using size 7 (4.5mm) needle. *Take time to check gauge..*

Bunny Mittens

Hop to it with these adorable kid-sized bunny mittens. Quick and easy to make, they'll have your little cottontail twitching with delight in no time.

DESIGNED BY SHERRY GRAZIANO

EASY

Sizes

Instructions are written for Child size Small. Changes for Medium are in parentheses.

Finished measurements

Hand circumference 5¼ (6)"/13.5 (15)cm
Length of cuff approx 3"/7.5cm

Materials

- 1 3½oz/100g ball (each approx 220yd/201m) of Cascade Yarns *220 Superwash* (superwash wool) each in #817 aran (MC) and #835 pink rose (CC)
- One set (5) size 6 (4mm) double-pointed needles (dpns) *or size to obtain gauge*
- Stitch markers
- Four ⅜"/9mm 4-hole shirt buttons in pink
- Tapestry needle

Stitch glossary

Kfb Knit in front and back of st—1 st increased.

Mitten (make 2)
CUFF

With dpns and MC, cast on 32 (36) sts and divide sts evenly over 3 needles. Join, taking care not to twist sts on needles, pm for beg of rnds. Work around in p2, k2 rib as foll:
Rnd 1 P1, k2, *p2, k2; rep from * around, end p1. Rep this rnd until piece measures 3"/7.5cm from beg.

HAND

Next (dec) rnd Knit, dec 3 sts evenly spaced around—29 (33) sts. Knit next 2 rnds. Cont in St st as foll:

THUMB GUSSET

Inc rnd 1 K 13 (15), pm, kfb, k1, kfb, pm, k to end—31 (35) sts. Knit next 2 rnds.
Inc rnd 2 K to first marker, sl marker, kfb, k3, kfb, sl marker, k to end—33 (37) sts. Knit next 2 rnds.
Inc rnd 3 K to first marker, sl marker, kfb, k5, kfb, sl marker, k to end—35 (39) sts. Knit next 1 (2) rnds.

FOR MEDIUM SIZE ONLY

Inc rnd 4 K to first marker, sl marker, kfb, k7, kfb, sl marker, k to end—41 sts. Knit next rnd.

FOR BOTH SIZES

Next rnd K to first marker, drop marker, place next 9 (11) sts on scrap yarn, drop marker, k to end—26 (30) sts. Cont in St st until piece measures 5½ (6¼)"/14 (16)cm from beg.

TOP SHAPING

Dec rnd 1 [K2, k2tog] 6 (7) times, k2—20 (23) sts. Knit next 2 rnds.
Dec rnd 2 [K1, k2tog] 6 (7) times, k2—14 (16) sts. Knit next rnd.
Dec rnd 3 [K2tog] 7 (8) times—7 (8) sts.
Dec rnd 4 K 1 (0), [k2tog] 3 (4) times—4 sts. Cut yarn, leaving a 6"/15cm tail and thread through rem sts. Pull tog tightly and secure end.

THUMB

Place 9 (11) thumb gusset sts over 2 needles.

Next rnd Join MC and knit across sts, then pick up and k 2 sts at base of hand—11 (13) sts. Divide sts evenly over 3 needles. Join and pm for beg of rnds. Cont in St st for 1 (1¼)"/2.5 (3)cm.

TOP SHAPING

Dec rnd 1 [K1, k2tog] 3 (4) times, k 2 (1)—8 (9) sts. Knit next rnd.
Dec rnd 2 [K2tog] 4 times, k 0 (1)—4 (5) sts. Cut yarn, leaving a 6"/15cm tail and thread through rem sts. Pull tog tightly and secure end.

EARS (make 4)

Beg at base of ear, with dpns and MC, cast on 5 sts. Working back and forth on 2 needles, work in garter st as foll:
Row 1 Knit.
Row 2 K1, M1, k to last st, M1, k1—7 sts.
(Continued on page 160.)

Gauge

20 sts and 28 rnds to 4"/10cm over St st using size 6 (4mm) dpns. *Take time to check gauge.*

Leaf-Lace Gauntlets

These elegant, lacy wristers make a strong fashion statement. They're knit back and forth in an intricate lace pattern that will entice and challenge even the experienced knitter.

DESIGNED BY JACQUELINE VAN DILLEN

EXPERIENCED

Sizes
Instructions are written for one size.

Finished measurements
Hand circumference 9"/23cm
Length approx 10¾"/27.5cm

Materials
■ 1 3½oz/100g hank (each approx 220yd/201m) of Cascade Yarns *220 Wool Heathers* (Peruvian highland wool) in #2452 turtle

■ One pair size 6 (4mm) needles *or size to obtain gauge*

Notes
1) Chart shows WS rows only.
2) As you work rows, the number of sts increase and decrease. You will beg with 41 sts and end with 41 sts.

Gauntlets (make 2)
Cast on 41 sts. Knit next 4 rows.
Beg chart pat
Row 1 (WS) Work 41 sts.
Row 2 and all RS rows K the knit sts and p the purl sts; for each single yo, work p1; for side-by-side yo's, work p1 in first yo, then p1 tbl in 2nd yo. Cont in this way to top of chart (row 53), then rep row 2. Knit next 5 rows.
Bind off all sts knitwise.

Finishing
Sew seams. For left gauntlet thumb opening, place piece seam side up on work surface. Position seam so it is 1¾"/4.5cm from top left side edge; mark with a pin. Tack top edge at pin mark. For right gauntlet thumb opening, place piece seam side up on work surface. Position seam so it is 1¾"/4.5cm from top right side edge; mark with a pin. Tack top edge at pin mark. ■

Gauge
18 sts and 22 rows to 4"/10cm over chart pat using size 6 (4mm) needles.
Take time to check gauge.

46 Leaf-Lace Gauntlets

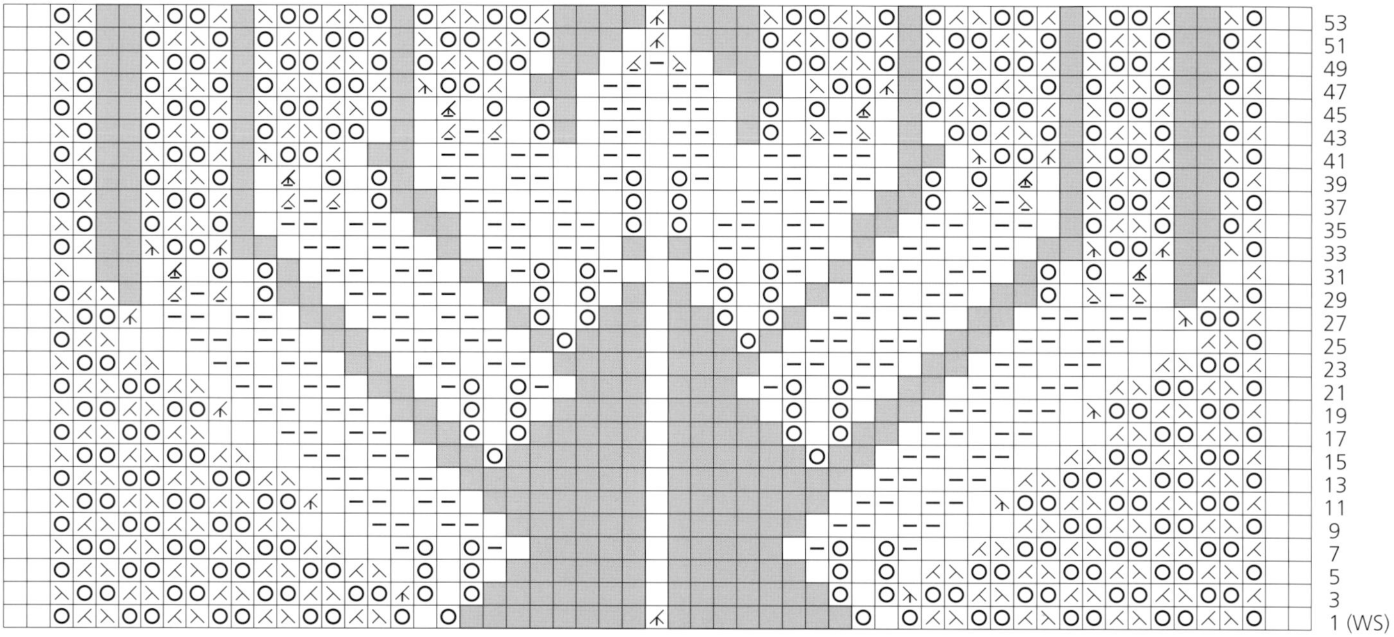

53
51
49
47
45
43
41
39
37
35
33
31
29
27
25
23
21
19
17
15
13
11
9
7
5
3
1 (WS)

Stitch Key

- K on WS
- P on WS
- No stitch
- Yo
- K2tog
- Ssk
- P2tog
- P2tog tbl
- K3tog
- S2KP
- P3tog

Quick Tip
As with any pattern, it's beneficial to read the chart all the way through before casting on to avoid surprises!

Striped & Ruffled Wrap

Splashes of color flow from a seed-stitch border, which provides the perfect frame for this vibrant ruffled scarf. This more advanced knit will reward your patience with a wearable work of art.

DESIGNED BY ANGELA JUERGENS

EXPERIENCED

Finished measurements
Approx 8¼" x 45"/21cm x 114.5cm

Materials
■ 1 3½oz/100g hank (each approx 220yd/201m) of Cascade Yarns *220 Wool Heathers* (Peruvian highland wool) each in #9561 seafoam heather (A), #2436 mimosa (B), #2435 japanese maple (C), #2439 gelato (D) and #2451 nectarine (E)

■ One pair size 7 (4.5mm) needles *or size to obtain gauge*

Stitch glossary
Lifted purl inc (inc 1 p-st)
Use RH needle to pull up the loop of the last st of the row below and place it on LH needle. Purl this st.

Short-row wrapping
(wrap and turn—w&t)
RIGHT SIDE
1) Work specified number of sts on chart.
2) Wyib, slip next st knitwise onto RH needle.
3) Wyif, slip st back onto LH needle (one wrapped st), turn to WS (leaving rem sts unworked) and work to end of next (WS) row foll chart.
4) On chart rows that are marked with a star, work as foll: *Work to wrapped st. Insert RH needle under the wrap and place it on LH needle. Knit it tog with next stitch on LH needle*. Rep from * to end of row.

Gauge
20 sts and 28 rows to 4"/10cm over St st using size 7 (4.5mm) needles.
Take time to check gauge.

Striped & Ruffled Wrap

Moss stitch
Row 1 (RS) *K1, p1;
rep from * to end.
Row 2 Rep row 1.
Row 3 *P1, k1; rep from * to end.
Row 4 Rep row 3.
Rep rows 1–4 for moss st.

Ruffle
With A, cast on 5 sts.
Beg chart pat
Row 1 (RS) K5.
Row 2 P5, inc 1 p-st—6 sts.
Row 3 K6.
Row 4 P6, inc 1 p-st—7 sts.
Row 5 K5, w&t.
Row 6 P5, inc 1 p-st—6 sts.
Row 7 K4, w&t.
Row 8 P4, inc 1 p-st—5 sts.

Row 9 K4, w&t.
Row 10 P4, inc 1 p-st—5 sts.
Row 11 Knit to end, picking up all
wraps—10 sts.
Row 12 P10, inc 1 p-st—11 sts. Cont
to foll chart in this way to row 147.
Rep rows 40–147 8 times, then work
rows 148–238 once. Bind off.

Neckband
With C, cast on 18 sts. Work even in
moss st until piece measures
45"/114.5cm from beg. Bind off in
moss st.

Finishing
Block pieces lightly to measurements.
Sew straight edge of ruffle to
neckband, easing in any fullness. ∎

Quick Tip
To help keep your place while knitting from a chart, place a
sticky note on the row above the one you're working.

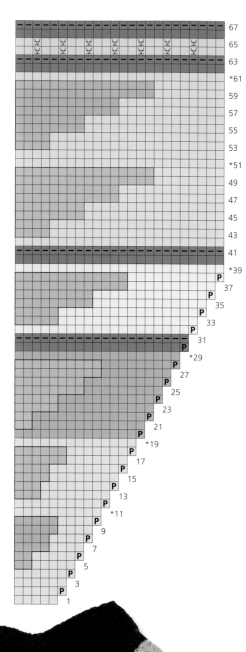

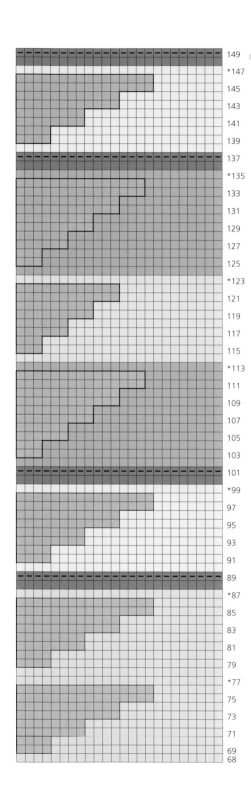

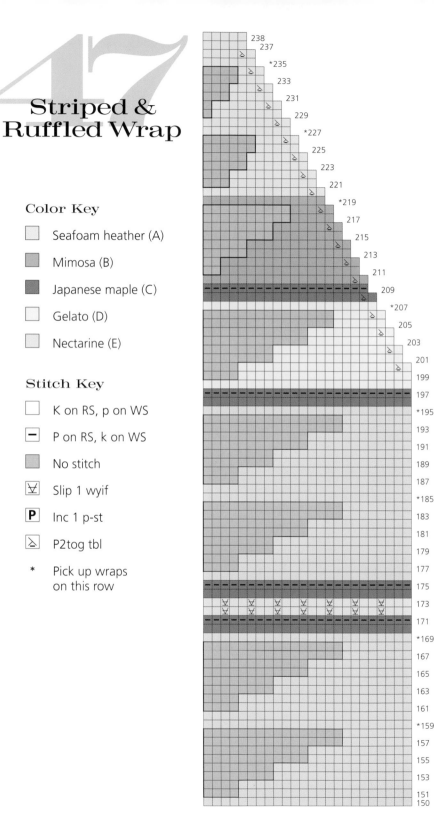

Striped & Ruffled Wrap

Color Key

- ☐ Seafoam heather (A)
- ▨ Mimosa (B)
- ▧ Japanese maple (C)
- ☐ Gelato (D)
- ▨ Nectarine (E)

Stitch Key

- ☐ K on RS, p on WS
- − P on RS, k on WS
- ▨ No stitch
- ⊻ Slip 1 wyif
- **P** Inc 1 p-st
- ◲ P2tog tbl
- * Pick up wraps on this row

48

Starfish Hat

The crown of this topper forms a pretty starfish shape. Adorned with bobbles and lace and knit in a warm golden shade, this sunny hat will brighten anyone's day.

DESIGNED BY ANNE FARNHAM

INTERMEDIATE

Sizes
Instructions are written for one size.

Finished measurements
Circumference 20"/51cm
(slightly stretched)
Depth 8¾"/22cm

Materials
■ 1 3½oz/100g hank (each approx 220yd/201m) of Cascade Yarns *220 Wool* (Peruvian highland wool) in #9463B gold
■ Size 4 and 6 (3.5 and 4mm) circular needles, 16"/40cm length *or size to obtain gauge*
■ One set (5) size 6 (4mm) double-pointed needles (dpns)
■ Stitch marker

Note To work in the rnd, always read chart from right to left

Stitch glossary
Make bobble K1, p1, k1 in same st, making 3 sts from one; turn. P3, turn. K3, turn. P3, turn. SK2P.

Twisted rib panel
(worked over 5 sts)
Rnd 1 [P1, k1 tbl] twice, p1.
Rep rnd 1 for twisted rib panel.

Hat
With smaller circular needle, cast on 100 sts. Join and pm, taking care not to twist sts on needle. Work in k1, p1 rib for 1"/2.5cm.

Gauge
20 sts and 28 rnds to 4"/10cm over St st using larger circular needle.
Take time to check gauge.

Starfish Hat

The lovely starfish motif on the top is a fun surprise.

Next (inc) rnd *K10, M1; rep from * around—110 sts. Change to larger circular needle. Work in St st for 5 rnds.
Beg chart pat and twisted rib panel
Rnd 1 *Work chart over next 17 sts, work twisted rib panel over next 5 sts; rep from * around. Cont to foll chart and twisted rib panel in this way to rnd 8.
Next rnd *K17, work twisted rib panel over next 5 sts; rep from * around. Rep last rnd until piece measures 7½"/19cm from beg.

CROWN SHAPING
Change to dpns (dividing sts evenly between 4 needles) when there are too few sts on circular needle.
Dec rnd 1 *Ssk, knit to 2 sts before twisted rib panel, k2tog, work twisted rib panel over next 5 sts; rep from * around—100 sts. Rep dec rnd 1 *every* rnd until 3 sts rem between twisted rib panels—40 sts.
Dec rnd 2 *SK2P, work twisted rib panel; rep from * around—30 sts.
Dec rnd 2 *P2tog, [k1 tbl, p1] twice; rep from * around—25 sts.
Dec rnd 3 *Ssk, k2tog, p1; rep from * around—15 sts.
Dec rnd 4 [K2tog] 7 times, k1—7 sts. Cut yarn, leaving an 8"/20.5cm tail and thread through rem sts. Pull tog tightly and secure end. ■

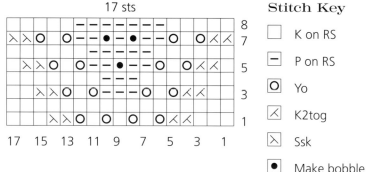

17 sts

17 15 13 11 9 7 5 3 1

Stitch Key

☐	K on RS
—	P on RS
O	Yo
⟋	K2tog
⟍	Ssk
●	Make bobble

Quick Tip
If you're after an even slouchier look, extend the section before the crown shaping begins by a few more rows.

Slip-Stitched Hat

Slip into fall in this slip-stitched number. The diamond pattern and rich burgundy hue evoke the beauty of autumn leaves.

DESIGNED BY ALEXANDRA TINSLEY

INTERMEDIATE

Sizes
Instructions are written for size Small/Medium. Changes for Large are in parentheses.

Finished measurements
Circumference 20 (21½)"/51 (54.5)cm
Depth Depth 8¾ (9)"/22 (23)cm

Materials
■ 1 3½oz/100g hank (each approx 220yd/201m) of Cascade Yarns *220 Wool* (Peruvian highland wool) in #8895 christmas red

■ Size 7 (4.5mm) circular needle, 16"/40cm length *or size to obtain gauge*

■ One set (4) size 7 (4.5mm) double-pointed needles (dpns)

■ Stitch marker

Garter stitch
Rnd 1 Purl.
Rnd 2 Knit.
Rep rnds 1 and 2 for garter st.

Slip-stitch pattern
(multiple of 8 sts)
Rnd 1 *K1, sl 7 wyif; rep from * around.
Rnd 2 Knit.

Rnd 3 K4, *insert RH needle under loose strand from rnd 1 and k next st on LH needle, bringing st out under strand, k7; rep from * around, end last rep k3 (instead of k7).
Rnd 4 K to last 3 sts, sl 3 wyif.
Rnd 5 Sl 4 wyif (cont from rnd 4), k1, *sl 7 wyif, k1; rep from * to last 3 sts, end k3.
Rnd 6 Knit.
Rnd 7 *Insert RH needle under loose strand from rnd 5 and k next st on LH needle, bringing st out under strand, k7; rep from * around.
Rnd 8 Knit.
Rep rnds 1–8 for slip st pat.

Hat
With circular needle, cast on 104 (112) sts. Join and pm, taking care not to twist sts on needle. Work in garter st for 8 rnds. Cont in sl st pat, rep rnds 1–8 6 times. Cont in St st as foll:

CROWN SHAPING
Change to dpns (dividing sts evenly between 3 needles) when there are too few sts on circular needle.
Dec rnd 1 *K 11 (12), k2tog; rep from * around—96 (104) sts. Knit next rnd.
Dec rnd 2 *K 10 (11), k2tog; rep from * around—88 (96) sts. Knit next rnd.

Dec rnd 3 *K 9 (10), k2tog; rep from * around—80 (88) sts. Knit next rnd.
Dec rnd 4 *K 8 (9), k2tog; rep from * around—72 (80) sts. Knit next rnd.
Dec rnd 5 *K 7 (8), k2tog; rep from * around—64 (72) sts. Knit next rnd.
Dec rnd 6 *K 6 (7), k2tog; rep from * around—56 (64) sts. Knit next rnd.
Dec rnd 7 *K 5 (6), k2tog; rep from * around—48 (56) sts. Knit next rnd.
Dec rnd 8 *K 4 (5), k2tog; rep from * around—40 (48) sts. Knit next rnd.
Dec rnd 9 *K 3 (4), k2tog; rep from * around—32 (40) sts. Knit next rnd.
Dec rnd 10 *K 2 (3), k2tog; rep from * around—24 (32) sts. Knit next rnd.
Dec rnd 11 *K 1 (2), k2tog; rep from * around—16 (24) sts. Knit next rnd.

FOR LARGE SIZE ONLY
Dec rnd 12 *K1, k2tog; rep from * around—16 sts. Knit next rnd.

FOR BOTH SIZES
Next rnd [K2tog] 8 times—8 sts.
Cut yarn, leaving an 8"/20.5cm tail and thread through rem sts. Pull tog tightly and secure end. ■

Gauge
21 sts and 32 rnds to 4"/10cm over sl st pat using size 7 (4.5mm) circular needle. *Take time to check gauge.*

Ruffled Scarf

Add a hint of prestige to your wardrobe with this Tudor-inspired scarf. The rich broken-rib pattern and garter-stitch ruffles will have you feeling like royalty.

DESIGNED BY CATHY CARRON

INTERMEDIATE

Finished measurements
Approx 8" x 48"/20.5cm x 122cm

Materials
- 2 3½oz/100g hanks (each approx 220yd/201m) of Cascade Yarns *220 Wool Heathers* (Peruvian highland wool) in #9441 mauve heather
- One pair size 7 (4.5mm) needles *or size to obtain gauge*

Stitch glossary
Lifted inc Use RH needle to pull up the loop of the st of the row below and place it on LH needle. Knit this st, then knit the st on the LH needle.

Hurdle stitch
(multiple of 2 sts)
Rows 1 and 2 Knit.
Rows 3 and 4 *K1, p1; rep from * to end.
Rep rows 1–4 for hurdle st.

Scarf
FIRST RUFFLE
Cast on 184 sts.
Row 1 (RS) *K2tog; rep from * to end—92 sts.
Rows 2–19 Knit.
Row 20 *K2tog; rep from * to end—46 sts.

CENTER SECTION
Work even in hurdle st until piece measures 45"/114.5cm from beg, end with a WS row.

SECOND RUFFLE
Row 1 (RS) *Lifted inc; rep from * to end—92 sts.
Rows 2–19 Knit.
Row 20 *Lifted inc; rep from * to end—184 sts. Bind off all sts loosely knitwise.

Finishing
Block piece lightly to measurements. ■

Gauge
23 sts and 30 rows to 4"/10cm over hurdle st using size 7 (4.5mm) needles.
Take time to check gauge.

Cabled-Cuff Mittens

Cabled cuffs turn ordinary mitts into extraordinary accessories. You'll knit the cabled band first, then pick up stitches along the top to complete the mitten for a design that goes every which way.

DESIGNED BY CHERYL MURRAY

◼◼◼◻
INTERMEDIATE

Sizes
Instructions are written for one size.

Finished measurements
Hand circumference 7"/17.5cm
Length of cuff approx 3¼"/8cm

Materials
◾ 1 3½oz/100g hank (each approx 220yd/201m) of Cascade Yarns *220 Wool* (Peruvian highland wool) in #8412 pear

◾ Contrasting heavy worsted-weight yarn (waste yarn)

◾ One set (5) size 6 (4mm) double-pointed needles (dpns) *or size to obtain gauge*

◾ Cable needle (cn)

◾ Size G/6 (4mm) crochet hook (for chain-st provisional cast-on)

Stitch markers

Stitch glossary
4-st RPC Sl 2 sts to cn and hold to *back*, k2, p2 from cn.
4-st LPC Sl 2 sts to cn and hold to *front*, p2, k2 from cn.
4-st RC Sl 2 sts to cn and hold to *back*, k2, k2 from cn.
4-st LC Sl 2 sts to cn and hold to *front,* k2, k2 from cn.
M1R (make 1 right) Insert LH needle from *back* to *front* into the strand between last st worked and the next st on the LH needle. Knit into the front loop to twist the st.
M1L (make 1 left) Insert LH needle from *front* to *back* into the strand between last st worked and the next st on the LH needle. Knit into the back loop to twist the st.

Left mitten
CUFF
With crochet hook and waste yarn, ch 24 for chain-st provisional cast-on. Cut yarn and draw end though lp on hook. Turn ch so bottom lps are at top and cut end is at left. With dpn and main yarn, beg 2 lps from right end, pick up and k 1 st in each of next 20 lps.

Beg chart pat
Row 1 (RS) Beg at st 1 and work to st 20. Working back and forth on 2 dpns, cont to foll chart in this way to row 20, then rep rows 1–20 once more, then rows 1–19 once. With RS facing, release cut end from lp of waste yarn ch. Pulling out 1 ch at a time, place live sts on a dpn. Graft ends tog using Kitchener st or 3-needle bind-off, forming a ring.

HAND
With RS facing, pick up and k 40 sts evenly spaced around one edge of cuff, beg and ending at joining, and dividing sts evenly over 4 needles. Join and pm for beg of rnds. Purl next 3 rnds for reverse St st ridge.

THUMB GUSSET
Inc rnd 1 K10, pm, M1, pm, k to end—41 sts. Knit next 2 rnds.
Inc rnd 2 K to first marker, sl marker, M1L, k1, M1R, sl marker, k to end—43 sts. Knit next 2 rnds.
Inc rnd 3 K to first marker, sl marker, M1L, k3, M1R, sl marker, k to end—45 sts. Knit next 2 rnds.
Inc rnd 4 K to first marker, sl marker, M1L, k5, M1R, sl marker, k to end—47 sts. Knit next 2 rnds.

Gauge
22 sts and 33 rnds to 4"/10cm over St st using size 6 (4mm) dpns.
Take time to check gauge.

Cabled-Cuff Mittens

Inc rnd 5 K to first marker, sl marker, M1L, k7, M1R, sl marker, k to end—49 sts. Knit next 2 rnds.

Inc rnd 6 K to first marker, sl marker, M1L, k9, M1R, sl marker, k to end—51 sts. Knit next 2 rnds.

Inc rnd 7 K to first marker, sl marker, M1L, k11, M1R, sl marker, k to end—53 sts. Knit next 2 rnds.

Next rnd K to first marker, drop marker, place next 13 sts on scrap yarn for thumb, drop marker, cast on 1 st, k to end—41 sts. Cont in St st until piece measures approx 4½"/11.5cm above reverse St st ridge, dec 1 st at end of rnd—40 sts.

TOP SHAPING

Dec rnd 1 *K8, k2tog; rep from * around—36 sts. Knit next rnd.

Dec rnd 2 *K7, k2tog; rep from * around—32 sts. Knit next rnd.

Dec rnd 3 *K6, k2tog; rep from * around—28 sts. Knit next rnd.

Dec rnd 4 *K5, k2tog; rep from * around—24 sts. Knit next rnd.

Dec rnd 5 *K4, k2tog; rep from * around—20 sts. Knit next rnd.

Dec rnd 6 *K3, k2tog; rep from * around—16 sts. Knit next rnd.

Dec rnd 7 *K2, k2tog; rep from * around—12 sts. Knit next rnd.

Dec rnd 8 *K1, k2tog; rep from * around—8 sts.

Dec rnd 9 [K2tog] 4 times—4 sts. Cut yarn, leaving a 6"/15cm tail and thread through rem sts. Pull tog tightly and secure end.

THUMB

Place 13 thumb gusset sts over 2 needles.

Next rnd Join yarn and knit across sts, then pick up and k 1 st in cast-on of thumb opening—14 sts. Divide sts evenly over 3 needles. Join and pm for beg of rnds. Cont in St st for 1"/2.5cm.

TOP SHAPING

Dec rnd 1 [K2tog, k3] twice, k2tog, k2—11 sts. Knit next rnd.

Dec rnd 2 [K2tog, k2] twice, k2tog, k1—8 sts. Knit next rnd.

Dec rnd 3 [K2tog, k1] twice, k2tog—5 sts. Cut yarn leaving a 6"/15cm tail and thread through rem sts. Pull tog tightly and secure end.

Finishing

CUFF EDGING

With RS facing and dpns, pick up and k 40 sts evenly spaced around, beg and ending at joining. Join and pm for beg of rnds. Purl next 3 rnds for reverse St st ridge. Bind off all sts purlwise.

Right mitten

Work as for left mitten to thumb gusset.

THUMB GUSSET

Inc rnd 1 K30, pm, M1, pm, k to end—41 sts. Knit next 2 rnds. Beg with inc rnd 2, cont to work as for left mitten. ■

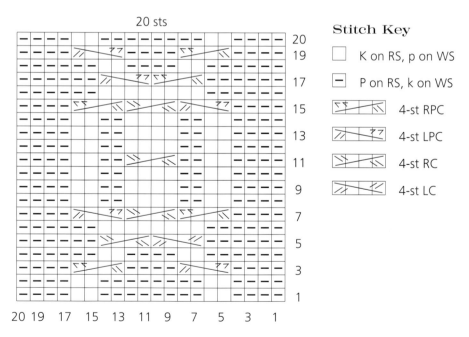

20 sts

Stitch Key

☐ K on RS, p on WS

─ P on RS, k on WS

4-st RPC

4-st LPC

4-st RC

4-st LC

Cabled Scarf Hat

What's even cozier than a scarf and a hat? A scarf hat! Pompom-topped and edged with fringe, this playful accessory wraps around your neck for extra warmth.

DESIGNED BY GALINA CARROLL

■■■■
EXPERIENCED

Sizes
Instructions are written for one size.

Finished Measurements
Circumference 21"/53.5cm
Depth 8½"/21.5cm (excluding scarf ties)

Materials
■ 1 3½oz/100g hank (each approx 220yd/201m) of Cascade Yarns *220 Wool Heathers* (Peruvian highland wool) each in #2423 mont martre (MC) and #9345 wisteria (CC)

■ One pair size 8 (5mm) needles *or size to obtain gauge*

■ Size 7 and 8 (4.5 and 5mm) circular needles, 16"/40cm length

■ One set (5) size 7 (4.5mm) double-pointed needles (dpns)

■ Cable needle (cn)

■ Size H/8 (5mm) crochet hook (for fringe)

■ Stitch holders

■ Stitch marker

Notes
1) Scarf ties are worked back and forth following chart pat and hat is worked in the rnd following the same chart pat.

2) To work in the rnd, always read chart from right to left.

Stitch glossary
3-st RPC Sl 1 st to cn and hold to *back*, k2, p1 from cn.
3-st LPC Sl 2 sts to cn and hold to *front*, p1, k2 from cn.
3-st RC Sl 1 st to cn and hold to *back*, k2, k1 from cn.
3-st LC Sl 2 sts to cn and hold to *front*, k1, k2 from cn.
4-st RC Sl 2 sts to cn and hold to *back*, k2, k2 from cn.
4-st LC Sl 2 sts to cn and hold to *front*, k2, k2 from cn.

MAKE BOBBLE A
Working in horizontal strand between last st made on RH needle and next st on LH, work (p1, k1, p1) making 3 sts into strand; turn. K3, turn. P3tog (1 st rem), p next st on LH needle, pass 1 st from the p3tog over p-st just made.

MAKE BOBBLE B
P1, k1, p1 in same st, making 3 sts from one; turn. K3, turn. P3tog.

Hat
SCARF TIES (make 2)
With straight needles and CC, cast on 22 sts. Knit next 2 rows. Change to MC.
Beg chart pat I
Row 3 (RS) Beg at st 1 and work to st 22. Cont to foll chart in this way to row 30, then rep rows 1–30 twice more. Place sts on holder ready for a RS rnd.

FRONT BRIM
With straight needles and MC, cast on 44 sts. Knit next 2 rows. Place sts on holder ready for a RS rnd.

BACK BRIM
With straight needles and MC, cast on 22 sts. Knit next 2 rows. Place sts on holder ready for a RS rnd.

Gauge
22 sts and 26 rows to 4"/10 cm over chart pat using size 8 (5mm) needles. *Take time to check gauge.*

52 Cabled Scarf Hat

SIDES
Place sts on larger circular needle as foll: first scarf tie, front brim sts, 2nd scarf tie and back brim sts—110 sts. Join yarn and cont in the rnd as foll:

Beg chart pat I

Rnd 1 Rep sts 1–22 5 times. Join and pm for beg of rnds. Cont to foll chart in this way to rnd 30. Change to smaller circular needle and work rnds 1–9.

CROWN SHAPING
Dec rnd 1 *P1, k1, ssk, k1, p2, k2, p1, p2tog, p1, k2, p2, k1, ssk, k1, p1; rep from * around 4 times more—95 sts.

Beg chart pat II

Rnd 1 Beg at st 1 and work to st 19. Cont to foll chart in this way to row 4.

Dec rnd 2 *P1, SK2P, p2tog, ssk, p3tog, ssk, p2tog, SK2P, p1; rep from * around 4 times—45 sts.

Next rnd *P1, [k1, p1] 4 times; rep from * around 4 times more. Rep this rnd twice more.

Dec rnd 3 *P1, [ssk] 4 times; rep from * around 4 times more—25 sts. Cut yarn, leaving an 8"/20.5cm tail and thread through rem sts. Pull tog tightly and secure end.

Finishing
Block piece lightly to measurements.
FRINGE
Cut 8"/20.5cm lengths of CC. Using 3 strands for each fringe, attach 7 fringe evenly spaced across each end of scarf tie (see page 37). Trim ends evenly.
Using CC, make a pompom 1½"/4cm in diameter. Sew pompom to top of hat. ■

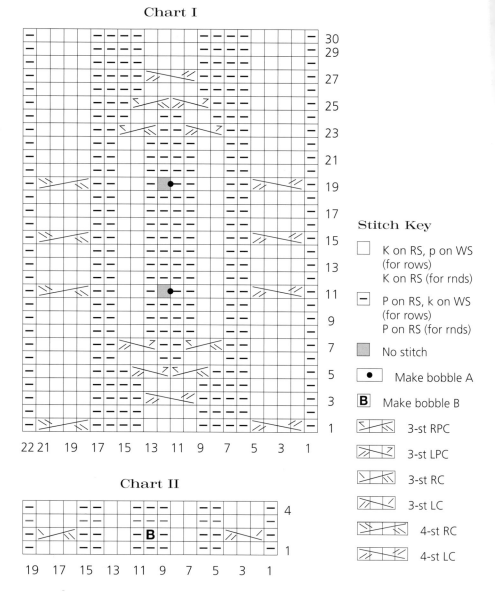

Chart I

Chart II

Stitch Key

☐ K on RS, p on WS (for rows)
K on RS (for rnds)

— P on RS, k on WS (for rows)
P on RS (for rnds)

▨ No stitch

● Make bobble A

B Make bobble B

3-st RPC

3-st LPC

3-st RC

3-st LC

4-st RC

4-st LC

Two-Color Slip-Stitched Hat

Knit in two shades of green, this colorful cap is perfect for a stroll in the woods. Slip-stitched colorwork and a naturally rolling brim add pizzazz to the simple shape.

DESIGNED BY HELEN SHARP

INTERMEDIATE

Sizes
Instructions are written for one size.

Finished measurements
Circumference 19½"/49.5cm
Depth 7¾"/19.5cm

Materials
■ 1 3½oz/100g hank (each approx 220yd/201m) of Cascade Yarns *220 Wool Heathers* (Peruvian highland wool) each in #9410 celtic green (A) and #9407 celery (B)

■ One pair size 7 (4.5mm) needles *or size to obtain gauge*

Hat
With A, cast on 97 sts. Work in St st for 8 rows. Cont in pat sts and color sequence as foll:
Row 1 (RS) With B, k1, *sl 1 wyib, sl 1 wyif, sl 1 wyib, k1; rep from * to end.
Row 2 With B, p1, *sl 3 wyib, yo, p1; rep from * to end.
Row 3 With A, knit across dropping yo's to create loose strands in front of work.
Row 4 With A, purl.
Row 5 With B, k1, *sl 1 wyib, insert RH needle under loose strand from row 3 and k next st on LH needle, bringing st out under strand, sl 1 wyib, k1; rep from * to end.
Row 6 With B, k1, *sl 1 wyif, p1, sl 1 wyif, k1; rep from * to end.
Row 7 With A, knit.
Row 8 With A, purl.
Row 9 With B, k1, *sl 1 wyif, k1; rep from * to end.
Row 10 With B, purl.
Rows 11–20 Rep rows 1–10, reversing color sequence by using A instead of B, and B instead of A.
Rows 21–40 Rep rows 1–20 foll same color sequence.

CROWN SHAPING
Row 1 (RS) *[K1 A, k1 B] twice, with A ssk; rep from *, end k1 A—81 sts.
Row 2 Purl across foll same color sequence of row below.
Row 3 *K1 A, k1 B, k1 A, with A ssk; rep from *, end k1 A—65 sts.
Row 4 Rep row 2.
Row 5 *K1 A, k1 B, with A ssk; rep from *, end k1 A—49 sts.
Row 6 Rep row 2.
Row 7 *K1 A, with A ssk; rep from *, end k1 A—33 sts.
Row 8 With A, purl.
Row 9 *With A, ssk; rep from *, end k1—17 sts.
Row 10 With A, purl.
Row 11 *With A, ssk; rep from *, end k1—9 sts.
Row 12 With A, purl.
Row 13 *With A, ssk; rep from *, end k1—5 sts. Cut yarn, leaving an 18"/45.5cm tail and thread through rem sts. Pull tog tightly, secure end, then sew back seam. ■

Gauge
20 sts and 28 rnds to 4"/10cm over St st using size 7 (4.5mm) needles.
Take time to check gauge.

Twisted-Rib Hat

This blushing beauty puts a twist on a classic corrugated cap. If you'd like to switch things up, try a bolder hue or a serene tweed.

DESIGNED BY CATHY CARRON

INTERMEDIATE

Sizes
Instructions are written for one size.

Finished measurements
Circumference 20"/51cm (slightly stretched)
Depth 7½"/19cm

Materials
■ 2 3½oz/100g hanks (each approx 220yd/201m) of Cascade Yarns *220 Wool Heathers* (Peruvian highland wool) in #9442 baby rose heather

■ Size 10 (6mm) circular needle, 16"/40cm length or size to obtain gauge

■ One set (4) size 10 (6mm) double-pointed needles (dpns)

■ Stitch marker

■ Tapestry needle

Notes
1) Use a double strand of yarn throughout.
2) Hat is made from the top of the crown down.

Stitch glossary
Lifted inc Use RH needle to pull up the loop of the st of the rnd below and place it on LH needle. Knit this st, then knit the st on the LH needle.

Hat
CROWN
With dpns and 2 strands of yarn held tog, cast on 12 sts, leaving a long tail for sewing. Divide sts over 3 needles. Join, taking care not to twist sts on needles, pm for beg of rnds.
Rnd 1 Knit.
Rnd 2 [Lifted inc] 12 times—24 sts.
Rnd 3 Knit.
Rnd 4 *K1, lifted inc; rep from * around—36 sts.
Rnd 5 Knit.
Rnd 6 *Lifted inc; rep from around—72 sts.

Rnd 7 Knit.
Rnd 8 Rep rnd 4—108 sts. Change to circular needle.
Rnd 9 Knit.

SIDES
Work around in k3, p3 rib until piece measures 6½"/16.5cm from top of crown.
Next (dec) rnd *K3tog tbl, p3; rep from * around—72 sts. Work around in k1, p1 rib for 4 rnds. Bind off loosely in rib pat.

Finishing
Thread beg tail of hat in tapestry needle. Weave tail around opening at top of crown. Pull tog tightly and secure end. ■

Gauge
22 sts and 19 rnds to 4"/10cm over k3, p3 rib using double strand of yarn and size 10 (6mm) needle. *Take time to check gauge.*

Triple-Cable Scarf

Every knitter needs a classic cabled scarf. Knit this traditional warmer in a bright color to add modern appeal to a knitterly classic.

DESIGNED BY DEBBIE O'NEILL

EXPERIENCED

Finished measurements

Approx 7½" x 57"/19cm x 144.5cm

Materials

- 2 3½oz/100g hanks (each approx 220yd/201m) of Cascade Yarns *220 Wool* (Peruvian highland wool) in #9495 harvest
- One pair size 8 (5mm) needles *or size to obtain gauge*
- Cable needle (cn)
- Stitch markers

Stitch glossary

3-st RPC Sl 1 st to cn and hold to *back*, k2, p1 from cn.
3-st LPC Sl 2 sts to cn and hold to *front*, p1, k2 from cn.
4-st RC Sl 2 sts to cn and hold to *back*, k2, k2 from cn.
4-st LC Sl 2 sts to cn and hold to *front*, k2, k2 from cn.
6-st RC Sl 3 sts to cn and hold to *back*, k3, k3 from cn.
6-st LC Sl 3 sts to cn and hold to *front*, k3, k3 from cn.
M1 p-st With the needle tip, lift the strand between the last st worked and the next st on the LH needle and purl it.
Wrap 6 sts 4 times Over the next 6 sts work k2, p2, k2, then slip them to cn and hold to *front*, wrap yarn *around* sts from front to back 4 times, return sts to RH needle.

Seed stitch

(over an odd number of sts)
Row 1 (RS) K1, *p1, k1; rep from * to end.

Row 2 K the purl sts and p the knit sts. Rep row 2 for seed st.

Scarf

Cast on 43 sts. Work in seed st for 6 rows.

Set-up row (WS) Work first 5 sts in seed st, pm, k2, p1, M1 p-st, p2, M1 p-st, p1, k6, p2, M1 p-st, p1, k2, M1, k1, p1, M1 p-st, p2, k6, p1, M1 p-st, p2, M1 p-st, p1, k2, pm, work last 5 sts in seed st—50 sts.

Beg chart pat

Row 1 (RS) Work in seed over first 5 sts, work 40 sts of chart, work in seed st over last 5 sts. Cont to foll chart in this way to row 24, then rep rows 1–24 until piece measures approx 56"/142cm from beg, end with row 1 or 17.

Next (dec) row (WS) Work in seed st over first 5 sts, drop marker, k2, p2tog, p2, p2tog, k6, p1, p2tog, p1, k1, k2tog, k1, p1, p2tog, p1, k6, p2tog, p2, p2tog, k2, drop marker, work in seed st over last 5 sts—43 sts. Work in seed st for 6 rows. Bind off in all sts knitwise.

Finishing

Block piece lightly to measurements. ■

Quick Tip

The seed-stitch border on this beauty creates density which allows the scarf to lie flat. Otherwise, the edges would curl.

Gauge

18 sts and 26 rows to 4"/10cm over St st using size 8 (5mm) needles.
Take time to check gauge.

55 Triple-Cable Scarf

40 sts

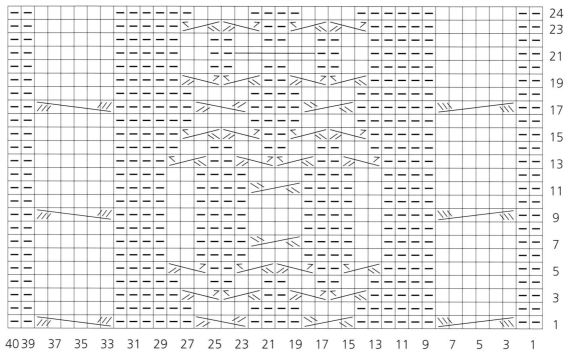

40 39 37 35 33 31 29 27 25 23 21 19 17 15 13 11 9 7 5 3 1

Stitch Key

☐	K on RS, p on WS
—	P on RS, k on WS
⊼⊼	3-st RPC
⊼⊼	3-st LPC
⊼⊼	4-st RC
⊼⊼	4-st LC
⊼⊼⊼	6-st RC
⊼⊼⊼	6-st LC
⊞⊞	Wrap 6 sts 4 times

Flip-Top Mittens

Perfect for the knitter on the go, these lace-cuffed mittens have a fold-over flap.
Keep the tops closed for extra warmth or flip them open for finger mobility.

BY PATTI PIERCE STONE

Sizes
Instructions are written for one size.

Finished measurements
Hand circumference 6½"/16.5cm
Length of cuff approx 2½"/6.5cm

Materials
■ 1 3½oz/100g hank (each approx 220yd/201m) of Cascade Yarns *220 Wool Quatro* (Peruvian highland wool) in #9537 cedar tweed
■ One set (4) size 5 (3.75mm) double-pointed needles (dpns) *or size to obtain gauge*
■ Stitch markers
■ Tapestry needle

Note
The popovers (that turn wristers into mittens) are optional.

Stitch glossary
M1R (make 1 right) Insert LH needle from *back* to *front* into the strand between last st worked and the next st on the LH needle. Knit into the front loop to twist the st.
M1L (make 1 left) Insert LH needle from *front* to *back* into the strand between last st worked and the next st on the LH needle. Knit into the back loop to twist the st.

Lace stitch (multiple of 8 sts)
Rnd 1 K1, ssk, yo, k1, yo, k2tog, k1, p1.
Rnd 2 K1, yo, ssk, k1, k2tog, yo, k1, p1.
Rnd 3 K2, yo, S2KP, yo, k2, p1.
Rep rnds 1–3 for lace st I.

Lace stitch II (multiple of 9 sts)
Rnd 1 K1, ssk, yo, k1, yo, k2tog, k1, p2.
Rnd 2 K1, yo, ssk, k1, k2tog, yo, k1, p2.
Rnd 3 K2, yo, S2KP, yo, k2, p2.
Rep rnds 1–3 for lace st II.

Right Mitten
CUFF
With dpns, cast on 40 sts. Divide sts over 3 needles. Join, taking care not to twist sts on needles, pm for beg of rnds.
Purl one rnd, knit one rnd. Cont in lace st I until piece measures 2½"/6.5cm from beg, end on rnd 3.
Next rnd K16, pm, k1, ssk, yo, k1, yo, k2tog, k1, pm, k17.
Next rnd K16, sl marker, k1, yo, ssk, k1, k2tog, yo, k1, slip marker, k17.
Next (inc) rnd K to first marker, inc 2 sts evenly spaced, sl marker, k2, yo, S2KP, yo, k2, sl marker, k to end, inc 1 st evenly spaced—43 sts.

Gauge
24 sts and 28 rnds to 4"/10 cm over St st using size 5 (3.75mm) dpns.
Take time to check gauge.

Flip-Top Mittens

THUMB GUSSET

Rnd 1 K18, sl marker, M1R, k1, ssk, yo, k1, yo, k2tog, k1, M1L, sl marker, k18—45 sts.

Rnd 2 K18, sl marker, k2, yo, ssk, k1, k2tog, yo, k2, sl marker, k18.

Rnd 3 K18, sl marker, k3, yo, S2KP, yo, k3, sl marker, k18.

Rnd 4 K18, sl marker, M1R, k2, ssk, yo, k1, yo, k2tog, k2, M1L, sl marker, k18—47 sts.

Rnd 5 K18, sl marker, k3, yo, ssk, k1, k2tog, yo, k3, sl marker, k18.

Rnd 6 K18, sl marker, k4, yo, S2KP, yo, k4, sl marker, k18.

Rnd 7 K18, sl marker, M1R, k3, ssk, yo, k1, yo, k2tog, k3, M1L, sl marker, k18—49 sts.

Rnd 8 K18, sl marker, k4, yo, ssk, k1, k2tog, yo, k4, sl marker, k18.

Rnd 9 K18, sl marker, k5, yo, S2KP, yo, k5, sl marker, k18.

Rnd 10 K18, sl marker, M1R, k4, ssk, yo, k1, yo, k2tog, k4, M1L, sl marker, k18—51 sts.

Rnd 11 K18, sl marker, k5, yo, ssk, k1, k2tog, yo, k5, sl marker, k18.

Rnd 12 K18, sl marker, k6, yo, S2KP, yo, k6, sl marker, k18.

Rnd 13 K18, sl marker, k5, ssk, yo, k1, yo, k2tog, k5, sl marker, k18.

Rnds 14 and 15 Rep rnds 11 and 12.

Rnds 16–18 Rep rnds 13–15.

Next rnd K18, drop marker, place next 15 sts on scrap yarn for thumb, drop marker, k to end—36 sts. Divide sts over 3 needles (12 sts on each).

HAND

Popover placement (optional)
Cont in St st until piece measures 6¼"/16cm from beg.

Next rnd P18, k18.

For both styles
Cont in St st until piece measures 7"/17.5cm from beg. Work in lace st II for ¾"/2cm. Bind off all sts purlwise as foll: *p2tog, return new st to LH needle; rep from * around. Fasten off last st.

THUMB

Place 15 thumb gusset sts on dpns, dividing sts evenly over 3 needles (5 sts on each). Join yarn, leaving a long tail for sewing.

Rnd 1 K5, ssk, yo, k1, yo, k2tog, k5, pick up and k 1 st at base of thumb—16 sts. Join and pm for beg of rnds.

Rnd 2 K5, yo, ssk, k1, k2tog, yo, k6.

Rnd 3 K6, yo, S2KP, yo, k7.

Rnd 4 K5, ssk, yo, k1, yo, k2tog, k6.

Rnds 5 and 6 Rep rnds 2 and 3. Bind off all sts purlwise as foll: *p2tog, return new st to LH needle; rep from * around. Fasten off last st. Use yarn tail at base of thumb to close up any gap between thumb and hand.

POPOVER

With dpn, cast on 20 sts, with back of mitten facing and finger opening at top, pick up and k 1 st in each of 18 p-sts—38 sts. Divide sts evenly over 3 needles. Join, taking care not to twist sts on needles, pm for beg of rnds.

Rnd (inc) 1 K22, M1, k to last 2 sts, M1, k2—40 sts.

Rnds 2–7 K2, [p1, k2] 6 times, k20. Cont in St st until piece measures 2 ¼"/5.5cm from beg.

TOP SHAPING

Dec rnd 1 [K8, k2tog] 4 times—36 sts. Knit next rnd.

Dec rnd 2 [K7, k2tog] 4 times—32 sts. Knit next rnd.

Dec rnd 3 [K6, k2tog] 4 times—28 sts. Knit next rnd.

Dec rnd 4 [K5, k2tog] 4 times—24 sts. Knit next rnd.

Dec rnd 5 [K4, k2tog] 4 times—20 sts. Knit next rnd.

Dec rnd 6 [K3, k2tog] 4 times—16 sts. Knit next rnd.

Dec rnd 7 [K2, k2tog] 4 times—12 sts. Knit next rnd.

Dec rnd 8 [K1, k2tog] 4 times—8 sts. Cut yarn, leaving a 6"/15cm tail. Thread tail in tapestry needle, then thread through rem sts. Pull tog tightly and secure end.

Left mitten

Work as for right mitten to popover placement.

Popover placement (optional)
Cont in St st until piece measures 6¼"/16cm from beg.

Next rnd K18, p18. Cont to work as for right mitten. ∎

Drop-Stitch Neck Wrap

Brighten up your winter wardrobe with this vibrantly colored, buttoned wrap. Knit in an easy-to-memorize pattern with a simple allover repeat, this neck warmer is all about drape and movement.

DESIGNED BY AMY POLCYN

INTERMEDIATE

Finished measurements
Approx 11" x 39"/28cm x 99cm

Materials
■ 2 3½oz/100g hanks (each approx 220yd/201m) of Cascade Yarns *220 Wool Heathers* (Peruvian highland wool) in #2428 framboise
■ One pair size 8 (5mm) needles *or size to obtain gauge*
■ One 1½"/38mm button

Drop-stitch pattern
(multiple of 10 sts plus 6)
Rows 1 and 2 Knit.
Row 3 (RS) K6, *yo twice, k1, yo 3 times, k1, yo 4 times, k1, yo 3 times, k1, yo twice, k6; rep from * to end.
Row 4 Knit to end, dropping extra wraps.
Rows 5 and 6 Knit.

Row 7 K1, *yo twice, k1, yo 3 times, k1, yo 4 times, k1, yo 3 times, k1, yo twice, k6; rep from *, end last rep k1 (instead of k6).
Row 8 Rep row 4.
Rep rows 1–8 for drop st pat.

Head scarf
Cast on 46 sts. Knit next 2 rows. Work in drop st pat until piece measures approx 38½"/97.5cm from beg, end with row 2. Knit next 2 rows. Bind off all sts knitwise.

Finishing
Block piece lightly to measurements. On RS, sew on button approx 9"/23cm from one end and centered side to side. To fasten, insert button through long loops of dropped sts. ■

Gauge
17 sts and 20 rows to 4"/10cm over drop stitch pattern using size 8 (5mm) needles.
Take time to check gauge.

Spotted Fair Isle Mittens

You won't mind seeing spots with these trompe l'oeil mitts. Knit with only two colors, they look much more complex thanks to the variegated yarn.

DESIGNED BY CHERYL MURRAY

INTERMEDIATE

Sizes
Instructions are written for one size.

Finished measurements
Hand circumference 8"/20.5cm
Length of cuff approx 2¾"/7cm

Materials
■ 1 3½oz/100g hank (each approx 220yd/201m) of Cascade Yarns *220 Paints* (Peruvian highland wool) in #9859 tropical punch (MC)

■ 1 3½oz/100g hank (each approx 220yd/201m) of Cascade Yarns *220 Wool* (Peruvian highland wool) in #8400 charcoal grey (CC)

■ Contrasting heavy worsted-weight yarn (waste yarn)

■ One set (5) size 6 (4mm) double-pointed needles (dpns) *or size to obtain gauge*

■ Stitch marker

■ Tapestry needle

Note
To work in the rnd, always read charts from right to left.

Corrugated rib
(multiple of 2 sts)
Rnd 1 *K1 with CC, p1 with MC; rep from * around.
Rep rnd 1 for corrugated rib.

Right mitten
CUFF
With dpns and CC, cast on 52 sts. Divide sts over 4 needles (13 sts on each). Join, taking care not to twist sts on needles, pm for beg of rnds.
Next rnd Purl.
Next rnd *K1 with CC, k1 with MC; rep from * around. Cont in corrugated rib for 14 rnds. With CC, knit one rnd, purl one rnd, knit one rnd. Cont in St st as foll:

HAND
Beg chart pat I
Rnd 1 Rep sts 1–26 twice. Cont to foll chart in this way through rnd 21.

THUMB PLACEMENT
Rnd 22 Work first 2 sts foll chart, k7 onto waste yarn, sl these 7 sts back to LH needle; beg with st 3 of chart, knit these 7 sts again, then work to end of rnd. Cont to foll chart through rnd 43.

TOP SHAPING
Rnds 44–54 Work to top of chart, working decs as indicated—8 sts. Cut CC leaving a 6"/15cm tail. Thread tail in tapestry needle, then thread through rem sts. Pull tog tightly and secure end. Cut and weave in MC on WS.

THUMB
Remove waste yarn and place 14 live sts on dpns as foll: 7 sts below thumb opening on needle 2 and 7 sts above opening on needle 4.
Beg chart pat II
Rnd 1 Work sts 1–10 twice as foll: with RS facing, needle 1 and CC, pick up and k 2 sts along RH edge of thumb opening (taking care to leave space for one more st to be picked up at end of rnd), beg

Gauge
26 sts and 28 rnds to 4"/10cm over chart pat using size 6 (4mm) dpns.
Take time to check gauge.

Spotted Fair Isle Mittens

Chart I

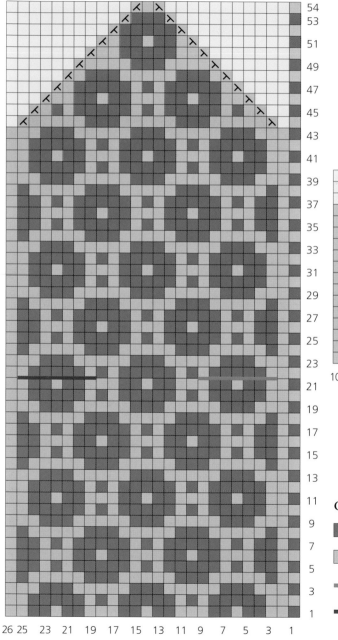

54
53
51
49
47
45
43
41
39
37
35
33
31
29
27
25
23
21
19
17
15
13
11
9
7
5
3
1

26 25 23 21 19 17 15 13 11 9 7 5 3 1

Stitch Key

☐ No stitch

⟋ K2tog

⟍ Ssk

Chart II

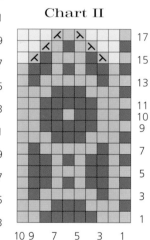

17
15
13
11
10
9
7
5
3
1

10 9   7   5   3   1

Color Key

■ Tropical punch (MC)

▨ Charcoal grey (CC)

▬ Right thumb placement

▬ Left thumb placement

with st 3, work to st 9 over next 7 sts on needle 2, with needle 3 and CC, pick up and k 3 sts along LH edge of thumb opening, beg with st 3, work to st 9 over next 7 sts on needle 4, with needle 4 and CC, pick up and k 1 st along LH edge of thumb opening—20 sts. Join and pm for beg of rnds. Divide sts evenly between 4 needles.
Cont to foll chart, rep sts 1–10 twice, through rnd 14.

TOP SHAPING
Rnds 15–17 Work to top of chart, working decs as indicated—8 sts. Cut CC, leaving a 6"/15cm tail. Thread tail in tapestry needle, then thread through rem sts. Pull tog tightly and secure end. Cut and weave in MC on WS. Use yarn tail at base of thumb to close up gap between thumb and hand.

Left mitten
Work as for right mitten to rnd 22 (thumb placement).

THUMB PLACEMENT
Rnd 22 Work first 18 sts foll chart, k7 onto waste yarn, sl these 7 sts back to LH needle; beg with st 19 of chart, knit these 7 sts again, then work to end of rnd. Cont to work as for right mitten. ■

Hugs & Kisses Mittens

Whip up these mittens for a Valentine's Day stroll with your sweetie. The classic XOXO cable combined with mock cabling on the back and the vibrant red color will get your heart beating.

DESIGNED BY LYNN WILSON

EXPERIENCED

Sizes
Instructions are written for one size.

Finished measurements
Hand circumference 7"/17.5cm
Length of cuff approx 2¾"/7cm

Materials
■ 1 3½oz/100g hank (each approx 220yd/201m) of Cascade Yarns *220 Wool* (Peruvian highland wool) in #9466 zinnia red
■ One set (5) size 7 (4.5mm) double-pointed needles (dpns) *or size to obtain gauge*
■ Cable needle (cn)
■ Stitch markers
■ Tapestry needle

Stitch glossary
C3B 3-st RC Sl 1 st to cn and hold to *back,* k2, k1 from cn.
C3F 3-st LC Sl 2 sts to cn and hold to *front,* k1, k2 from cn.
C4B 4-st RC Sl 2 sts to cn and hold to *back,* k2, k2 from cn.
C4F 4-st LC Sl 2 sts to cn and hold to *front,* k2, k2 from cn.

LT (left twist) With RH needle behind LH needle, skip next st on LH needle; knit 2nd st tbl, then knit skipped st in front lp, sl both sts from LH needle.

Left mitten
CUFF
With dpns, cast on 40 sts. Divide sts over 4 needles (10 sts on each). Join, taking care not to twist sts on needles, pm for beg of rnds. Cont in rib pat as foll:
Rnds 1–3 P1, *k2, p2; rep from * around, end k2, p1.
Rnd 4 P1, *LT, p2; rep from * around, end LT, p1. Rep rnds 1–4 four times more. Cont in pat sts and beg thumb gusset as foll:

THUMB GUSSET
Rnd 1 P1, [k2, p2] 4 times, k2, p1, pm, M1 p-st, pm, p1, k2, p1, k1, p1, k8, p1, k1, p1, k2, p1—41 sts.
Rnd 2 P1, [k2, p2] 4 times, k2, p1, slip marker, p1, slip marker, p1, k2, p1, k1, p1, k8, p1, k1, p1, k2, p1.
Rnd 3 P1, [k2, p2] 4 times, k2, p1, slip marker, M1 p-st, p1, M1 p-st, slip marker, p1, k2, p1, k1, p1, k8, p1, k1, p1, k2, p1—43 sts.

Gauge
20 sts and 26 rnds to 4"/10 cm over St st using size 7 (4.5mm) dpns.
Take time to check gauge.

Hugs & Kisses Mittens

Rnd 4 P1, [LT, p2] 4 times, LT, p1, slip marker, p to next marker, slip marker, p1, LT, p1, k1, p1, 4-st LC, 4-st RC, p1, k1, p1, LT, p1.

Rnd 5 P1, [k2, p2] 4 times, k2, p1, slip marker, p to next marker, slip marker, p1, k2, p1, k1, p1, k8, p1, k1, p1, k2, p1.

Rnd 6 P1, [k2, p2] 4 times, k2, p1, slip marker, M1 p-st, pl to next marker, M1 p-st, slip marker, p1, k2, p1, k1, p1, k8, p1, k1, p1, k2, p1—45 sts.

Rnd 7 Rep rnd 5.

Rnd 8 P1, [LT, p2] 4 times, LT, p1, slip marker, p to next marker, slip marker, p1, LT, p1, k1, p1, 4-st RC, 4-st LC, p1, k1, p1, LT, p1.

Rnd 9 Rep rnd 6—47 sts.

Rnds 10 and 11 Rep rnd 5.

Rnd 12 P1, [LT, p2] 4 times, LT, p1, slip marker, M1 p-st, p to next marker, M1 p-st, slip marker, p1, LT, p1, k1, p1, 4-st RC, 4-st LC, p1, k1, p1, LT, p1—49 sts.

Rnd 13 and 14 Rep rnd 5.

Rnd 15 Rep rnd 6—51 sts.

Rnd 16 Rep rnd 4.

Rnd 17 Rep rnd 5.

Rnd 18 Rep rnd 6—53 sts (13 sts between thumb gusset markers).

Rnd 19 Rep rnd 5.

Rnd 20 Rep rnd 4.

Next rnd P1, [k2, p2] 4 times, k2, p1, drop marker, place next 13 sts on scrap yarn for thumb, drop marker, cast on 1 st, p1, k2, p1, k1, p1, k8, p1, k1, p1, k2, p1—41 sts.

HAND

Rnds 1 and 2 P1, [k2, p2] 4 times, k2, p3, k2, p1, k1, p1, k8, p1, k1, p1, k2, p1.

Rnd 3 P1, [LT, p2] 4 times, LT, p3, LT, p1, k1, p1, 4-st RC, 4-st LC, p1, k1, p1, LT, p1.

Rnds 4–6 Rep rnd 1.

Rnd 7 Rep rnd 3.

Rnds 8–10 Rep rnd 1.

Rnd 11 P1, [LT, p2] 4 times, LT, p3, LT, p1, k1, p1, 4-st LC, 4-st RC, p1, k1, p1, LT, p1.

Rnds 12–14 Rep rnd 1.

Rnd 15 Rep rnd 11.

Rnd 16 P1, [k2, p2] 4 times, k2, p2tog, p1, k2, p1, k1, p1, k8, p1, k1, p1, k2, p1—40 sts.

Rnds 17 and 18 P1, [k2, p2] 5 times, k2, p1, k1, p1, k8, p1, k1, p1, k2, p1.

Rnd 19 P1, [LT, p2] 5 times, LT, p1, k1, p1, 4-st RC, 4-st LC, p1, k1, p1, LT, p1.

Rnds 20–22 Rep rnd 17.

Rnd 23 Rep rnd 19.

Rnds 24–26 Rep rnd 17.

Rnd 27 P1, [LT, p2] 5 times, LT, p1, k1, p1, 4-st LC, 4-st RC, p1, k1, p1, LT, p1.

Rnds 28 and 29 Rep rnd 17.

TOP SHAPING

Rnd 30 P1, ssk, p2tog, [k2, p2tog] 3 times, ssk, p2, k1, [ssk] twice, k2, k2tog, ssk, k1, [ssk] twice, k2, p1—28 sts.

Rnd 31 K2tog, p1, [LT, p1] 3 times, k1, p2tog, LT, k1, 3-st LC, 3-st RC, k1, LT, p1—26 sts.

Rnd 32 [(Ssk) twice, k2tog] twice, p1, [ssk] twice, k2tog, ssk, [k2tog] twice, p1—14 sts. Cut yarn, leaving a 8"/20.5cm tail. Thread tail in tapestry needle, then thread through rem sts. Pull tog tightly and secure end.

THUMB

Place 13 thumb gusset sts on dpns, dividing sts evenly over 3 needles as foll: place first 4 sts on needle one, next 5 sts on needle 2 and last 4 sts on needle 3. Join yarn, leaving a long tail for sewing.

Next rnd Pick up and knit 1 st in cast-on st at base of thumb, M1 p-st, p to end, then M1 p-st—16 sts. Join and pm for beg of rnds. Purl next 11 rnds.

TOP SHAPING

Dec rnd 1 [P2, p2tog] 4 times—12 sts. Purl next rnd.

Dec rnd 2 [P1, p2tog] 4 times—8 sts. Cut yarn, leaving a 6"/15cm tail and thread through rem sts. Pull tog tightly and secure end. Use yarn tail at base of thumb to close up any gaps between thumb and hand.

Right mitten

Work as for left mitten to thumb gusset.

THUMB GUSSET

Rnd 1 P1, k2, p1, k1, p1, k8, p1, k1, p1, k2, p1, pm, M1 p-st, pm, p1, [k2, p2] 4 times, k2, p1—41 sts.

Rnd 2 P1, k2, p1, k1, p1, k8, p1, k1, p1, k2, p1, slip marker, p1, slip marker, p1, [k2, p2] 4 times, k2, p1.

Rnd 3 P1, k2, p1, k1, p1, k8, p1, k1, p1, k2, p1, slip marker, M1 p-st, p1, M1 p-st, slip marker, p1, [k2, p2] 4 times, k2, p1—43 sts.

Rnd 4 P1, LT, p1, k1, p1, 4-st LC, 4-st RC, p1, k1, p1, LT, p1, slip marker, p to next marker, slip marker, p1, [LT, p2] 4 times, LT, p1.

Rnd 5 P1, k2, p1, k1, p1, k8, p1, k1, p1, k2, p1, slip marker, p to next marker, slip marker, p1, [k2, p2] 4 times, k2, p1.

Rnd 6 P1, k2, p1, k1, p1, k8, p1, k1, p1, k2, p1, slip marker, M1 p-st, p to next marker, M1 p-st, slip marker, p1, [k2, p2] 4 times, k2, p1—45 sts.

Rnd 7 Rep rnd 5.

Rnd 8 P1, LT, p1, k1, p1, 4-st RC, 4-st LC, p1, k1, p1, LT, p1, slip marker, p to next marker, slip marker, p1, [LT, p2] 4 times, LT, p1.

Rnd 9 Rep rnd 6—47 sts.

Rnds 10 and 11 Rep rnd 5.

Rnd 12 P1, LT, p1, k1, p1, 4-st RC, 4-st LC, p1, k1, p1, LT, p1, slip marker, M1 p-st, p to next marker, M1 p-st, slip marker, p1, [LT, p2] 4 times, LT, p1—49 sts.

Rnds 13 and 14 Rep rnd 5.

Rnd 15 Rep rnd 6—51 sts.

Rnd 16 Rep rnd 4.

Rnd 17 Rep rnd 5.

Rnd 18 Rep rnd 6—53 sts (13 sts between thumb gusset markers).

Rnd 19 Rep rnd 5.

Rnd 20 Rep rnd 4.

Next rnd P1, k2, p1, k1, p1, k8, p1, k1, p1, k2, p1, drop marker, place next 13 sts on scrap yarn for thumb, drop marker, cast on 1 st, p1, [k2, p2] 4 times, k2, p1—41 sts.

HAND

Rnds 1 and 2 P1, k2, p1, k1, p1, k8, p1, k1, p1, k2, p3, [k2, p2] 4 times, k2, p1.

Rnd 3 P1, LT, p1, k1, p1, 4-st RC, 4-st LC, p1, k1, p1, LT, p3, [LT, p2] 4 times, LT, p1.

Rnds 4–6 Rep rnd 1.

Rnd 7 Rep rnd 3.

Rnds 8–10 Rep rnd 1.

Rnd 11 P1, LT, p1, k1, p1, 4-st LC, 4-st RC, p1, k1, p1, LT, p3, [LT, p2] 4 times, LT, p1.

Rnds 12–14 Rep rnd 1.

Rnd 15 Rep rnd 11.

Rnd 16 P1, k2, p1, k1, p1, k8, p1, k1, p1, k2, p2tog, p1, [k2, p2] 4 times, k2, p1—40 sts.

Rnds 17 and 18 P1, k2, p1, k1, p1, k8, p1, k1, p1, [k2, p2] 5 times, k2, p1.

Rnd 19 P1, LT, p1, k1, p1, 4-st RC, 4-st LC, p1, k1, p1, [LT, p2] 5 times, LT, p1.

Rnds 20–22 Rep rnd 17.

Rnd 23 Rep rnd 19,

Rnds 24–26 Rep rnd 17.

Rnd 27 P1, LT, p1, k1, p1, 4-st LC, 4-st RC, p1, k1, p1, [LT, p2] 5 times, LT, p1.

Rnds 28 and 29 Rep rnd 17.

TOP SHAPING

Rnd 30 P1, k1, [ssk] twice, k2, k2tog, ssk, k1, [ssk] twice, k2, p2, ssk, p2tog, [k2, p2tog] 3 times, ssk, p1—28 sts.

Rnd 31 P1, LT, k1, 3-st LC, 3-st RC, k1, LT, p2tog, k1, [p1, LT] 3 times, p1, ssk—26 sts.

Rnd 32 P1, [ssk] 3 times, [k2tog] 3 times, p1, [ssk] twice, k2tog, ssk, [k2tog] twice—14 sts. Cut yarn, leaving a 8"/20.5cm tail. Thread tail in tapestry needle, then thread through rem sts. Pull tog tightly and secure end.

THUMB

Work as for left mitten. ■

✳ **Quick Tip**
If you don't have a cable needle handy, you can use a spare double-pointed needle or even a chopstick!

Scandinavian Mittens

Your hands will be toasty all winter long in these multicolored, Norwegian-style warmers.
Put your colorwork skills to work and top off with pompoms for extra flare.

DESIGNED BY GALINA CARROLL

Sizes
Instructions are written for one size.

Finished measurements
Hand circumference 8"/20.5cm
Length of cuff approx 2½"/6.5cm
(excluding pompoms)

Materials
■ 1 3½oz/100g hank (each approx 220yd/201m) of Cascade Yarns *220 Wool* (Peruvian highland wool) each in #8555 black (A), #9476 maize (B), #4146 persimmon (C), #7815 summer sky (D) and #8339 marine (E)

■ Contrasting heavy worsted-weight yarn (waste yarn)

■ One set (5) size 8 (5mm) double-pointed needles (dpns) *or size to obtain gauge*

■ Stitch marker

■ Tapestry needle

Note
To work in the rnd, always read charts from right to left.

Right mitten
With dpns and A, cast on 40 sts. Divide sts over 4 needles (10 sts on each). Join, taking care not to twist sts on needles, pm for beg of rnds.
Beg chart pat I
Rnd 1 Rep sts 1–20 twice. Cont to foll chart in this way through rnd 22.

THUMB PLACEMENT
Rnd 23 Foll chart, k8 sts onto waste yarn, sl these 8 sts back to LH needle, knit these 8 sts again, then work to end of rnd. Cont to foll chart through rnd 42.

TOP SHAPING
Rnds 43–50 Work to top of chart, working decs as indicated—8 sts. Cut yarn, leaving a 6"/15cm tail. Thread tail in tapestry needle, then thread through rem sts. Pull tog tightly and secure end.

THUMB
Remove waste yarn and place 16 live sts on dpns as foll: 8 sts below thumb opening on needle 1 and 8 sts above opening on needle 3. Arrange sts on 3 dpns as foll: Place last 2 sts on needle 1 and first 2 sts in needle 3 on needle 2 (4 sts on each). Join D, leaving a long tail for sewing. Join and pm for beg of rnds.
Beg chart pat II
Rnd 1 Work sts 1–8 twice. Cont to foll chart in this way through rnd 11.

Gauge
20 sts and 22 rnds to 4"/10cm over chart pat using size 8 (5mm) dpns.
Take time to check gauge.

Scandinavian Mittens

Chart I

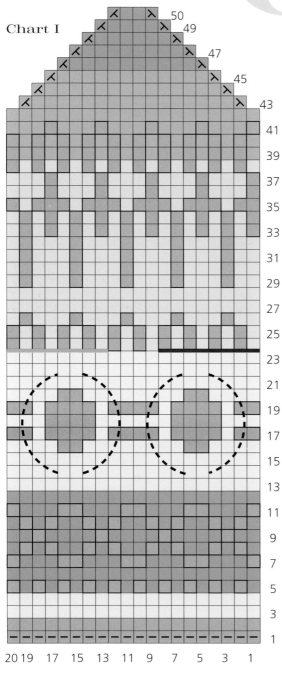

Chart II

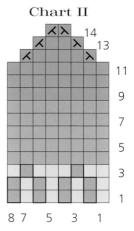

TOP SHAPING

Rnds 12–14 Work to top of chart, working decs as indicated—4 sts. Cut yarn, leaving a 6"/15cm tail. Thread tail in tapestry needle, then thread through rem sts. Pull tog tightly and secure end. Use yarn tail at base of thumb to close up any gaps between thumb and hand.

Left mitten

Work as for right mitten to rnd 23 (thumb placement).

THUMB PLACEMENT

Rnd 23 Work first 12 sts foll chart, k8 sts onto waste yarn, sl these 8 sts back to LH needle, knit these 8 sts again, then work to end of rnd. Cont to work as for right mitten.

Finishing

Referring to chart I, use A to embroider chain stitch (see page 24) half circles. Make 16 pompoms ¾"/2cm in diameter. Sew 6 pompoms evenly spaced around bottom edge of each cuff. Sew a pompom to top of each mitten and tip of each thumb. ■

Color Key

- Black (A)
- Summer sky (D)
- Persimmon (C)
- Marine (E)
- Maize (B)
- — Right thumb placement
- — Left thumb placement

Stitch Key

- K on RS
- — P on RS
- ⊼ K2tog
- ⋋ Ssk
- - - - Chain stitch

✱ Instructions (continued)

4
Puppy Mittens
continued from page 15

Next 2 rows K2tog, k to end. Bind off rem 3 sts.

Finishing
Working in satin stitch, using tapestry needle and CC, embroider a nose on tip of each mitten. Referring to photo, sew on ears and eyes.

TAIL
With RS facing, dpns and MC, pick up and k 4 sts at center bottom of cuff, as shown. Work in I-cord as foll: ***Next row (RS)** With 2nd dpn, k4, do not turn. Slide sts back to beg of needle to work next row from RS; rep from * until I-cord measures 3"/7.5cm from beg.
Dec row 1 K1, k2tog, k1, do not turn. Slide 3 sts back to beg of needle to work next row from RS. Work next row even.
Dec row 2 K1, k2tog, do not turn. Slide 2 sts back to beg of needle to work next row from RS. Work next row even.
Dec row 3 K2tog. Cut yarn, leaving a 6"/15cm tail and thread through rem sts. Pull tog tightly and secure end. ■

SATIN STITCH

28
Reverse Stockinette Mittens
continued from page 77

Next row (WS) Knit.
Next row (RS) [P2tog] 8 times—8 sts.
Cut yarn, leaving a 6"/15cm tail. Thread tail in tapestry needle, then thread through rem sts. Pull tog tightly and secure end.

Finishing
Sew thumb seam, then sew cast-on sts of thumb to cast-on sts at base of thumb. Sew side seam, using CC for cuff and MC for hand.

Left mitten
Work cuff as for right mitten until rib measures 2½"/6.5cm, end with RS row. Change to larger needles and MC.
Next row (WS) Work in rib to last st, inc 1 in last st—41 sts.

THUMB GUSSET
Set-up row (RS) P16, k1, p2, k1, p21. Cont to work as for right mitten. ■

Shop Pocket Watch (shown above) Item #02D08.04 Available at garrettwade.com or call 800-221-2942

33
Pocket Cap
continued from page 87

I-CORD KNOTTED BUTTON
With dpn and CC, cast on 4 sts, leaving a long tail for sewing. Work in I-cord as foll:
*Next row (RS) With 2nd dpn, k4, do not turn. Slide sts back to beg of needle to work next row from RS; rep from * until I-cord measures 2½"/6.5cm from beg. Cut yarn, leaving a 6"/15.5cm tail. Thread tail in tapestry needle, then thread through rem sts. Pull tog tightly and secure end; do not cut off excess tail. Thread beg tail in tapestry needle. Weave tail around opening at beg of I-cord. Pull tog tightly and secure end; do not cut off excess tail. Tie I-cord in a knot, then sew ends tog to secure. Sew on button. ■

45
Bunny Mittens
continued from page 117

Row 3 Rep row 2—9 sts.
Rows 4–10 Knit.
Row 11 K1, k2tog, k to last 3 sts, k2tog, k1—7 sts.
Row 12 Rep row 11—5 sts.
Rows 13 and 14 Knit.
Row 15 K2tog, k1, k2tog—3 sts. Cut yarn, leaving a 6"/15cm tail and thread through rem sts. Pull tog tightly and secure end.

Finishing
Working in satin stitch, using tapestry needle and CC, embroider a nose on tip of each mitten. For each ear, fold in half at base and make a few stitches to hold fold. Referring to photo, sew on ears. For each inner ear, cut an 8"/20.5cm length of CC. Thread in tapestry needle. From RS, insert needle through base of ear. Then insert needle up, approx ⅛"/.3cm from first stitch. Remove tapestry needle. Even up yarn ends, then tie in a square knot. Trim ends to ¼"/.5cm. Use tip of needle to separate yarn ply and make fluffy. Use CC to sew on button eyes. With MC, make 2 pompoms 1⅜"/3.5cm in diameter. Sew each pompom to center bottom of cuff. ■